JOB SATISFACTION OF B.ED. TEACHER EDUCATORS

JOB SATISFACTION OF B.ED. TEACHER EDUCATORS

By

Dr. N. Kishore

Department of Education
Sri Venkateswara University
Tirupati
Andhra Pradesh
(India)

DISCOVERY PUBLISHING HOUSE PVT. LTD.
NEW DELHI-110 002

Published by:
Tilak Wasan

DISCOVERY PUBLISHING HOUSE PVT. LTD.
4831/24, Ansari Road, Prahlad Street
Darya Ganj, New Delhi-110002 (India)
Phone: +91-11-23279245, 43764432
Fax: +91-11-23253475
E-mail: parul.wasan@gmail.com
discoverypublishinghouse@gmail.com
info@discoverypublishinggroup.com
web: www.discoverypublishinggroup.com

***First Edition:* 2011**
ISBN: 978-81-8356-791-6

Job Satisfaction of B.Ed. Teacher Educators

Printed at:
Shree Balaji Art Press
Delhi

Dedicated
to my
Beloved Parents

N. Subramanyam
&
N. Kanthamma

Foreword

The development of any nation depends mainly on the standards of its educational institutions. Education is the most powerful and effective instrument for inducing radical changes in the behaviour of students. Education is the process through which an individual is developed into individuality and a person into a personality. Education should be individualized and personalized to the at most and should constitute preparation for self learning.

The teacher occupies pivotal position in the system of Education. With good leadership and appropriate teaching aids, the teacher effectiveness can be enhanced. But the most ingenious plans of inspired administrators and the best array of instructional devises are of little avail if the teacher is ignorant, unskilled or indifferent. Thus, the success of any educational reform depends upon the quality of teachers and intern the quality of teaching depends to a large extent on the quality of Teacher Education.

"Of all the different factors which influence the quality of education and its contribution to national development, the quality, competence and character of teachers are undoubtedly the most significant. Nothing is more important than securing a sufficient supply of high quality recruits to the teaching profession, providing them with the best possible professional preparation and creating satisfactory conditions of work in which they can be fully effective" (*Kothari Education Commission, 1964-66*).

Teachers of the olden age were men of the highest calibre in society from the point of knowledge and spiritual progress.

He (The Teacher) has been called equal to Absolute (Brahma) himself and only that person is authorized to be a "GURU" who has gained Absolute Knowledge. But today the teacher occupies a relatively low social status. He as an individual or as a member of the group does not enjoy prestige accorded to the medicine, law and engineering profession. On the contrary teachers are typically regarded as impractical, idealists and ill-equipped persons to deal with the realities of the world affairs. Hence, they carry no weight in the present community.

Teacher Education is the backbone of an education system in a progressing nation and the teacher educator is the pivot in the system of education. Teacher educator is also a teacher. Obviously, the progress of a nation ultimately depends upon the quality of its teachers. It is also acclaimed beyond doubt that the teaching profession is the noblest of all professions. But it is an irony of fact that teaching is the most unattractive profession and teacher no longer occupies an honorable position in the society.

The teacher in India today "Suffers from poverty, neglect, indifference and insecurity". Financially they are poor; socially their status is low; professionally their task is a drudgery and administratively they are the worst affected. The Secondary Education Commission (1954) was painfully impressed by the fact, that the social status, the salaries and the general service conditions of teachers are far from satisfactory.

Number of Teacher Educators of the present day has no interest in their profession. Many of the Teacher Educators are made to work in colleges of education without providing even the minimum requirements of accommodation and equipment. Therefore, it is no doubt to say that Teacher Educators of present day have no interest in their profession. The most important point is the lack of recognition for the Teacher Educators in the society, compared to the doctors, lawyers, police or any other government servants. The

Teacher Educators are being neglected from recognition, indifference and insecurity both from the society and the government thus a noble profession is receiving ignorable comments.

Though there is considerable number of studies on job satisfaction of industrial workers, very few studies were found on job satisfaction of Teachers. The present investigation entitled job satisfaction of Teacher Educators of B.Ed colleges, undertaken by Dr. N. Kishore is a presage-process study in the area of job satisfaction. It is considered to strike at the combination of both psycho-sociological factors in the process of job satisfaction of Teacher Educators working in B.Ed colleges.

I am confident that the findings of this investigation are of great relevance to the Teacher Educators. The target readers of this book would include Teacher Educators, Pre-services teachers, instructional designers and educational administrators. I have no hesitation to say that all the above mentioned target groups will find this book very useful.

Dr. B. RAMACHANDRA REDDY

Professor

Department of Education

Sri Venkateswara University College of Arts

Tirupati – 517 502, A.P. India

Preface

Job satisfaction is a set of favorable or unfavorable feelings and emotions with which employees view their work. Job satisfaction typically refers to attitudes of a particular employee but assessments of individual employee's satisfaction can be averaged by looking at overall performance of all the members of an organization.

Studies on job satisfaction seem to have begun with the famous Hawthorne studies conducted by Elton Mayo at the Western Electric company in the 1920s. Most of the studies conducted so far are in industrial setting examining the effects of physical conditions and design of equipment etc., on job satisfaction and productivity. Elton Mayo and his co-workers started very much in this direction. During the course of their investigations, however they became convinced that factors of a social nature also affect job satisfaction and productivity. The human relations school was thus born, which saw the function of the industrial psychologist as seeking to improve the happiness of the worker, and through this to improve productivity. The implicit assumption of course was that the satisfied worker produced more.

"No pupil can rise above the level of its teacher". The statement made about the role and status of Teacher in the National Policy of Education, 1986 is, besides being commendable, an eye-opener to all of us who are engaged in the teaching profession. To provide quality Teacher Education at secondary level, Teacher Educators must maintain a high level of academic and professional competence so as to prepare the best teachers for our country's schools. Unless we Teacher Educators are in a position to provide worthwhile experiences to our pupil-teachers for realizing the stipulated Teacher Education objectives related to particular type of Teacher Education course, the task of any worthwhile quality Teacher Education could be futile by all means, we have to illuminate ourselves like a lamp having enough energy in the form of burning oil for lighting the mind and hearts of our pupil-teachers.

Can we really play the role of such illuminated lamps? Are the present Teacher Educators available in our Teacher Education institution capable of providing the needed quality Teacher Education? Here an attempt is made to seek answer to these questions in the contest of the competence of our Teacher Educators working in B.Ed colleges along with the existing conditions and practices available for educating them as Teacher Educators.

Teacher Educators have a key role in improvement of Education. Therefore, it is important that their best efforts be devoted to it. Since there is so much flexibility in the work they are required to do, and the manner in which they can do it, the contribution they make to the field depend on part of their involvement in their work and the satisfactions they derive from it.

The colleges of education in Andhra Pradesh are controlled by two types of managements – government and private. With the impact of privatization and the reservation policy in the government, minority and non-minority institutions are also there in this state.

The present study is to investigate the job satisfaction of Teacher Educators working in B.Ed colleges and also to know the relationship between the job satisfaction and job involvement. It is also aimed at to find the relation of job satisfaction of Teacher Educators with the various psycho-sociological variables. The relevant data from 592 Teacher Educators working in various B.Ed colleges in Andhra Pradesh were collected.

The book is presented in six chapters. In chapter I, brief introduction of the topic is given. Chapter II deals with a brief review of related literature. Chapter III deals with the present study. Chapter IV gives an account of methods employed in the investigation. Chapter V consists of analysis of data, results and discussion. The last one forms the summary, major findings, conclusions, educational implications, recommendations and suggestions for further research.

It is just fitness of things to state that this book is prepared to meet the requirements of Teacher Educators. I do not know to what extent I have succeeded in my attempt, but I will feel amply rewarded if this book can further the understanding of the concept 'Job satisfaction'. Any constructive suggestions for the betterment of this book will be greatly acknowledged.

Dr. N. KISHORE

Academic Consultant
(Teaching Assistant in Psychology)
Department of Education
Sri Venkateswara University College of Arts
Tirupati – 517 502, Andhra Pradesh, India.

Acknowledgements

I deem it a great privilege to express my beloved respects and deep sense of gratitude to my teacher and research supervisor Prof. B. Ramachandra Reddy, M.Sc., M.A., M.Ed., M.Phil., Ph.D., B.L., Diploma in Adult Education, Diploma in Statistics, Head and Chairman, Board of Studies, Department of Education, Srivenkateswara University, Tirupati, for his benevolent guidance and encouragement in the smooth conduct and completion of the study. I am greatly indebted to him for his inspiration, timely help and invaluable initiation.

I am highly thankful to Dr. D. Ramakrishnaiah, Professor in Education, Dr. V. Dayakara Reddy, Professor, and Principal of IASE; Dr. S. Padmanabaiah, Retd. Professor and Dr. M. Syamala, Associate Professor, Department of Education, Sri Venkateswara University, Tirupati, who have given valuable suggestions and helping-hand in completion of the investigation.

I wish to express my deep sense of appreciation to all the Research scholars, Teaching and Non-teaching staff of the Department of Education, Sri Venkateswara University, Tirupati, for giving me the source of strength and moral throughout the course of my study.

I am highly thankful to Dr. K. Sreenivasa Rao, Associate Professor; Dr. L.K. Reddy, Associate Professor and Dr. Viswanatha Reddy, Assistant Professor, Department of Psychology, S. V. University, for their valuable suggestions and kind co-operation for the completion of this investigation.

I sincerely wish to tender my heartful, gratitude to Prof. Y. Nirmala Jyothi, Sri Padmavathi Mahila Viswavidhyalayam; Dr. G. Vijayasree, Gr Asst, Lab Nursery School, Dept. of Home Science, S.V. University, Tirupati, and C. Manchala, S.A., M.P.U.P. School, Avilala, Tirupati for their constant encouragement and good wishes to complete this work.

I wish to express my thankfulness to B. Jayarami Reddy, Principal; Dr. Subramanyam, Professor; A. Sreenivasulu, A.O. and my colleagues, Annamacharya College of Education, at Rajampet, for unstrained help, constant encouragement and co-operation for the completion of this work.

I owe a lot to the generality and kindness of Prof. V. Kodanda Rami Reddy, Department of Econometrics, S.V. University, who helped a lot in statistical analysis of the data.

I place on record my special thanks to Principals and Teacher Educators in B.Ed. colleges in A.P, for and unstrained help, constant encouragement and co-operation in collecting research data.

I am particularly thankful to Dr. K. Subramanyam, Mr. Ranganath, Dr. Ranganswamy, S.S. Moses Isaiah, A. Ramanaiah, Bujji Sir, and K. Ramesh, Librarian, IASE, S.V.U., for their wishes and timely suggestions.

I am highly indebted to my wife T. Sudarsanamma, Gr, Asst, Lab Nursery School, Dept. of Home Science, S.V. University, Tirupati and sons Sri Koushik, Sri Karthik and also my sisters, Lakshmi, Sumalatha, Sudha and brother-in-laws, Sreenivas, Ram Narayana and my relatives for their affectionate blessing without which it could not be possible for me to complete this work.

I am thankful to Mr. G. Madhu, Sri Sai Graphics, Tirupati, to complete my thesis computer work without trouble.

Finally, I am thankful to all those who have helped me in completing this investigation.

N. Kishore

Contents

Abbreviation

JSI	-	Job Satisfaction Inventory
SDS	-	Socio Demographic Scale
JII	-	Job Involvement Inventory
SCS	-	Self Concept Scale
16PF	-	Cattell's Personality Questionnaire
DIET	-	District Institute of Education and Training
CTE	-	College of Teacher Education
IASE	-	Institutions of Advanced Study in Education
NCTE	-	National Council of Teacher Education
NPE	-	New Policy of Education
SCERT	-	State Council of Educational Research and Training
NCRT	-	National Council of Educational Research and Training
POA	-	Programme of Action
VN	-	Variable Number
UGC	-	University Grant Commission

CHAPTER 1

INTRODUCTION

MEANING OF EDUCATION

In its broadest meaning education is any process by which an individual gains knowledge, or insight, or develop attitudes or skills. Formal Education is acquired through organized study or instruction, as in a school or a college. Informal Education arises from day-to-day experiences or through relatively unplanned or undirected contacts with communications and media such as books, periodicals, motion pictures, radio or television. Function of education is both social and individual. Its social function is to help each individual become more effective member of society by passing along to him the collective experiences of the past and present. Its individual function is to enable him to lead a more satisfying and productive life by preparing him to handle new experiences successfully. Education is also the mane given to that science or branch of study that deals historically or contemporaneously with the principles and practices of teaching and learning.

From the beginning of modern education system Teacher education is a part and parcel of the formal educational system in India. It is intimately connected with society and is conditioned by the ethos, culture and character of a nation. The constitutional goals, the directive principles of the state policy, the socio-economic problems and the growth of knowledge, the emerging expectations and the changes operating in education, etc., call for an appropriate response from a futuristic education system and provide the perspective within which teacher education programmes need to be viewed.

When India attained freedom, the then existing educational system was accepted as such because it was thought that an abrupt departure from the same would be disturbing and destabilising. Thus a predisposition to retain the system acquired preponderance and all that was envisaged by way of changes was its rearrangement. Consequently, education including teacher education largely remained isolated from the needs and aspirations of the people. During the last five decades certain efforts have been made to indigenize the system. The gaps, however, are still wide and visible.

SYSTEM OF EDUCATION

India has a large system of education. There are nearly 5.98 lakh Primary Schools, 1.76 lakh Elementary Schools and 98 thousand High / Higher Secondary Schools in the country. Out of about 4.52 million teachers in the country nearly 3 million are teaching at the primary/ elementary level.

In pursuance of the NPE, 1986 a major step was taken by the Central Government to enhance the professional capacity of a large number of teacher education institutions. Nearly 430 District Institutes of Education and Training (DIETs) have already been established by 1997-98. The DIETs are charged with the responsibility of organising pre-service and in-service programmes in addition to being the nodal resource centers for elementary education at district level. Likewise, Colleges of Teacher Education (CTEs) and Institutions of Advanced Study in Education (IASEs) have been given the responsibility of introducing innovations in teacher education programmes at the secondary and higher secondary stages and in vocational education.

India has a large system of teacher education. There are more than 2000 elementary teacher education institutions,

Colleges of Education and University Departments of Education. Nearly 30,000 Teacher Educators are engaged in the preparation of school teachers. Due to the demand in the society NCTE is giving green signal to so many educational societies to run teacher education programmes. The number of colleges of education is increasing day by day in all most all states in India. In addition, there are Teacher Educators working in pre-primary training schools as well as in institutions concerned with the preparation of teachers for the education of children with special needs and alternative education such as non-formal education, distance education etc.

PROBLEMS OF THE NATION AND THE EXPECTED ROLE OF TEACHER EDUCATION

It is universally acknowledged that education is an effective means for social reconstruction and to a great extent it offers solutions to the problems a society is faced with. These problems may be economic, social, cultural, political, moral, ecological and educational. Since the teachers play a major role in education of children, their own education becomes a matter of vital concern. Teacher education must, therefore, create necessary awareness among teachers about their new roles and responsibilities.

Problems in this context of teacher education are:

1. Economic Problems
2. Social Problems
3. Problems of Cultural Reconstruction
4. Crises of Values and Morality

Economic Problems

Under-employment, poverty, and low rate of growth and productivity are some of the major economic problems of the country which have led to the compulsions of the backward economy. These problems seek immediate solution and demand a realistic co-ordination between economic planning and manpower planning. The Indian society needs education with special emphasis on science and technology, vocational inputs and realistic work experiences. Teacher education curriculum, therefore, has to promote such attitudes as are necessary for the emergence of a new economic order. The Teacher Educators should be in a position to prepare the teachers to understand the attributes of modernity and development.

Social Problems

Democracy, violence and terrorism cannot coexist. Casteism, communalism and regionalism are some of the problems in the society which misguide the youth. Increasing delinquency, violence, terrorism and fissiparous tendencies and use of inappropriate means to get one's ends are threats to the national integration and social cohesion. Education has to develop a peace-loving personality and the teacher educator has to function in this regard.

Problems of Cultural Reconstruction

Education is the process of transmission of dynamic and responsive components of cultural heritage and its continuous enrichment. There is a need to reinterpret the Indian culture in its distinct identity and composite strength. Its capacity to absorb the sublime from the other cultures needs to be highlighted. The teachers will have to play their role in cultural transmission and reconstruction. So the job of the Teacher Educators is a complex task in the present modernized world.

Crises of Values and Morality

There has been a persistent erosion of values in the society. In the present day context certain values need to be redefined and reinstalled. There are situations when the values imparted and inculcated in schools are not generally practised in society.

Strengthening national and social cohesion in a diverse and plural society, accelerating the process of economic growth, improving the life of the downtrodden and the people living below the poverty line, removing the widely prevalent ignorance, superstition and prejudices from the masses, inculcating scientific temper and developing a critical awareness about the social realities of Indian life are some of the issues which call for immediate attention. Teacher Educators and the teachers prepared by them have a special role to play in such efforts.

COMMISSIONS ON TEACHER EDUCATION IN INDIA

Various Commissions and Committees appointed by the Central and the State Governments in recent decades have invariably emphasised the need for quality teacher education suited to the needs of the educational system. The Secondary Education Commission (1953) observed that "a major factor responsible for the educational reconstruction at the secondary stage is teachers' professional training." The Education Commission (1964-66) stressed that "in a world based on science and technology it is education that determines the level of prosperity, welfare and security of the people" and that "a sound programme of professional education of teachers is essential for the qualitative improvement of education."

The Programme of Action (POA, 1992) has emphasised teacher education as a continuous process, its pre-service and in-service components being inseparable.

The POA, among others, has pointed out the following in respect of teacher education:

(a) Professional commitment and overall competencies of teachers leave much to be desired;

(b) The quality of pre-service education has not only improved with recent developments in pedagogical science, but has actually shown signs of deterioration;

(c) Teacher education programmes consist mainly of pre-service teacher training, with practically no systematic programmes of in-service training, facilities for which are lacking.

(d) There has been an increase in sub-standard institutions of teacher education and there are numerous reports of gross malpractices; and

(e) The support system provided by the State Councils of Educational Research and Training (SCERTs) and the University Departments of Education has been insufficient and there is no support system below the state level.

GENERAL OBJECTIVES OF TEACHER EDUCATION

The general objectives of teacher education derived from the contexts, concerns and issues of education, teacher education and the perceived profile of the teacher could include the following:

- To promote capabilities for inculcating national values and goals as enshrined in the Constitution of India.
- To enable teachers to act as agents of modernisation and social change.
- To sensitize teachers towards the promotion of social cohesion, international understanding and protection of human rights and rights of the child.
- To transform student-teachers into competent and committed professionals willing to perform the identified tasks.
- To develop competencies and skills needed for becoming an effective teacher.
- To sensitize teachers and Teacher Educators about emerging issues, such as environment, ecology, population, gender equality, legal literacy, etc..
- To empower teachers to cultivate rational thinking and scientific temper among students.
- To develop critical awareness about the social realities.
- To develop managerial and organisational skills.

TEACHER EDUCATION FOR SECONDARY STAGE

For teaching at secondary stage, the qualification most sought after is one year B.Ed. which is in fact B.Ed. for secondary stage. However, at present, there are several variations for first degree level qualification which are also available. These include B.Ed. (Elementary); B.Ed. (Special Education); which too are programmes of one year duration; B.Ed. through correspondence or distance education mode which is now of two years duration. There are certain other variations in the form of vacation courses or part-time courses which were available before NCTE norms came into force. In addition, there are four-year integrated courses for elementary stage and also for secondary stage.

Teacher education programme at this stage, like at all other stages, will include the theory, practice teaching in schools, and practical work in the light of contexts, concerns, profile of teachers and general and specific objectives.

Specific Objectives

The specific objectives at this stage may include the following:

- To enable the prospective teachers to understand the nature, purpose and philosophy of secondary education.
- To develop among teachers an understanding of the psychology of their pupils.
- To enable them to understand the process of socialisation.
- To equip them acquire competencies relevent to stage specific pedagogy, curriculum development, its transaction and evaluation.
- To enable them to make pedagogical analysis of the subjects they are to teach at the secondary stage.
- To develop skills for guidance and counselling.
- To enable them to foster creative thinking among pupils for reconstruction of knowledge.

- To acquaint them with factors and forces affecting educational system and classroom situation.
- To acquaint them with educational needs of special groups of pupils.
- To enable them to utilise community resources as educational inputs.
- To develop communication skills and use the modern information technology.
- To develop aesthetic sensibilities.
- To acquaint them with research in education including action research

PROFESSION

A Profession may be defined as an occupation based upon specialized, intellectual study and training. It is a work pursuit, one person's effort to find out a place in the work-a-day world. It is a kind of occupation which in bygone times, was termed as "Vocation" (Cook and Cook, 1930).

A favorable attitude towards any profession is likely to prove helpful to workers in maintaining harmonious relations with their colleagues, characterised by mutual affection and sympathetic understanding.

A profession is defined as "an occupation involving relatively long and specialized preparation on the level of the higher education and is governed by a special code of ethics" (Good, 1945).

Webster's New World Dictionary (1953) defined a profession as "A vocation or an occupation requiring advanced training in some liberal art or science and usually involving mental rather than manual work as teaching, engineering, writing etc".

Stinnet (1962) had defined a profession as "A Profession may be an occupation based upon specialized intellectual study and training, the purpose of which is to supply skilled service or advice to others for a definite fee or salary".

Peters et al. (1963) are of the opinion that "continuous in service growth has been identified as an important ingredient of professional people. Professional growth never ceases for the alert and dedicated teachers".

THE TEACHING PROFESSION

The role of the teacher in a society is well known. The well-being of the Nation depends upon the wellbeing of the teachers. The teacher has a powerful and abiding influence in the formation of the character of the future citizens. The teacher acts as a pivot for the transmission of intellectual and technical skills and cultural traditions from one generation to another.

The teaching profession should be intellectual, learning and practical activity. A strong, secure and effective profession of teaching is essential to build up public intelligence and to solve the social problems. Teachers who commit themselves to the profession and who have knowledge, devotion and sacrifice can only build teaching profession.

The primary obligation of the teaching profession is to guide children, youth and adults in pursuit of knowledge and skills to prepare them to the way of democracy which help them to become happy, useful, self supporting citizens. To fulfill this, the teacher should deal impartially regardless of their physical, mental, emotional, political, social, economical and religious characteristics.

The members of teaching profession should share with parents in shaping each student's purpose and get towards socially accepted needs. He has to respect the basic responsibility of parent for their children. He has to establish friendly and co-operative relationship with the home.

The teaching profession occupies a position of public trust involving not only the individual teacher's personal conduct but also the interaction of the school and the community. He should perform the duties of citizens and participate in community activities. He has to discuss controversial issues from an object point of view keeping the class from partisan opinions.

According to Best (1984), persons who choose teaching as a profession believed that teacher to be more secure, the profession to be less overcrowded, there was less physical strain, more opportunity for proper home life, more adequate lifetime income, it was easier to gain the needed education and there was less opposition from parents and others relatively than with certain other professions.

JOB SATISFACTION

Job satisfaction is in regard to one's feelings or state-of-mind regarding the nature of one's work. Job satisfaction can be influenced by a variety of factors, e.g., the quality of one's relationship with their supervisor, the quality of the physical environment in which they work, degree of fulfillment in their work, etc.

Job satisfaction describes how content an individual is with his or her job. It is a relatively recent term since in previous centuries the jobs available to a particular person were often predetermined by the occupation of that person's parent. There are a variety of factors that can influence a person's level of job satisfaction; some of these factors include the level of pay and benefits, the perceived fairness of the promotion system within a company, the quality of the working conditions, leadership and social relationships, and the job itself (the variety of tasks involved, the interest and challenge the job generates, and the clarity of the job description/requirements).

The happier people are within their job, the more satisfied they are said to be. Job satisfaction is not the same as motivation, although it is clearly linked. Job design aims to enhance job satisfaction and performance; methods include job rotation, job enlargement and job enrichment. Other influences on satisfaction include the management style and culture, employee involvement, empowerment and autonomous work groups. Job satisfaction is a very important attribute which is frequently measured by organisations. The most common way of measurement is the use of rating scales where employees report their reactions to their jobs. Questions relate to scale of pay, work responsibilities, variety of tasks, promotional opportunities, the work itself and co-workers.

Job satisfaction has been defined as a pleasurable emotional state resulting from the appraisal of one's job; an affective reaction to one's job; and an attitude towards one's job. Weiss (2002) has argued that job satisfaction is an attitude but points out that researchers should clearly distinguish the objects of cognitive evaluation which affect beliefs and behaviours. This definition suggests that we form attitudes towards our jobs by taking into account our feelings, our beliefs, and our behaviors.

TEACHERS AND SATISFACTION

Teachers of the olden age were men of the highest calibre in society from the point of knowledge and spiritual progress. He (The Teacher) has been called equal to Absolute (Brahma) himself and only that person is authorised to be a "GURU" who has gained Absolute Knowledge. But today the teacher occupies a relatively low social status. He as an individual or as a member of the group does not enjoy prestige accorded to the medicine, law and engineering profession. On the contrary teachers are typically recorded as impracticals, idealists and ill-equipped persons to deal with the realities of the world affairs. Hence, they carry no weight in the present community.

Teacher Education is the backbone of an education system in a progressing nation and the teacher educator is the pivot in the system of education. Teacher educator is also a teacher. Obviously, the progress of a nation ultimately depends upon the quality of its teachers. It is also acclaimed beyond doubt that the teaching profession is the noblest of all professions. But it is an irony of fact that teaching is the most unattractive profession and teacher no longer occupies an honourable position in the society. In this connection it is to quote the quotation of Mr. Henry Van Dyke, "He (the teacher) lives in obscurity and contents with hardship. For him trumphets blare, no chariots, no golden declarations are decreed...., patient in his duty, he quickens the indolence, encourages the eager and studies the unstable..... He lights many candles which in later years will shine back to cheer him". This is his reward.

The teacher in India today "suffers from poverty, neglect, indifference and insecurity". Financially they are poor; socially their status is low; professionally their task is a drudgery and administratively they are the worst affected. The Secondary Education Commission (1954) was painfully impressed by the fact, that the social status, the salaries and the general service conditions of teachers are far from satisfactory.

Number of Teacher Educators of the present day has no interest in their profession. Many of the Teacher Educators are made to work in colleges of education without providing even the minimum requirements of accommodation and equipment. Therefore, it is no doubt to say the Teacher Educators of present day have no interest in their profession. The most important point is the lack of recognition for the Teacher Educators in the society, compared to the doctors, lawyers, police or any other government servants. The Teacher Educators are being neglected from recognition, indifference and insecurity both from the society and the government thus a noble profession is receiving ignorable comments.

A dissatisfied teacher is lost not only to himself but also to the entire society. He spells disaster to the country's future. So dissatisfaction of an individual results in professional stagnation. If it occurs in the teaching profession, it is just suicidal. Pagel and Price (1980) listed different causes for the dissatisfaction of teachers. They are:

1. Lack of planning time
2. Too much correction work and clerical work
3. Out-of-touch administration
4. Disruptive and unmotivated students
5. Non-teaching activities
6. Non-cooperative parents
7. Feelings of failure and
8. Low occupational prestige.

JOB INVOLVEMENT

The concept of job involvement has been defined in various ways by different psychologists. Throughout the literature many different terms have been used to describe job involvement. Terms such as central life interests, work-role involvement, ego-involvement, ego-involved performance, occupational involvement, morale, intrinsic motivation, job satisfaction and job involvement have all been mentioned.

Job involvement was defined as "the degree to which a person's work performance affects his self-esteem" (Lodahl and Kejner, 1965). It is the degree to which a person is identified psychologically with his work, or the importance of work in his total self-image. Lodahl (1965) hypothesized that its main determinant is a value orientation process. A job involved person is one for whom work is a very important part of life, and is one who is affected very much personally by his whole job satisfaction, the work itself, his co-workers, the company etc.

On the other hand a non-job involved person does his living off the job. Work is not as important as a part of his psychological life. His interests are elsewhere and the core of his self-image, the essential part of his identity, is not greatly effected by the kind of work he does or how well he doesn't. A job involved person would like to come to his duty regularly, whereas a non job-involved person may not be regular, may absent himself from work, since his interests are elsewhere.

After review of all definitions of job involvement in psychological literature Robinowitz and Hall (1977) concluded that the definitions of job involvement should be grouped into two categories, each representing a distinct way of conceptualizing the construct.

One category of definitions views job involvement as a "performance self esteem" contingency. According to these definitions, job involvement is the extent to which the self-esteem of individuals is affected by their level of performance at work. Thus, higher or lower job involvement means higher or lower self-esteem derived from work behavior.

The other category of definitions views job involvement as a "component of self-image". According to this category of definitions, job involvement refers to the degree to which individuals identify themselves psychologically with their jobs.

CAUSES OF JOB INVOLVEMENT

Researchers who have defined job involvement as form of the performance self-esteem contingency argue that intrinsic need satisfaction is a necessary condition for job involvement. Vroom (1962) proposed that a person's attempts to satisfy the need for self-esteem through work on the job leads to job involvement. In his study Vroom found that the degree of job involvement by his choice of ego rather than extrinsic factors help in describing the sources of satisfaction and dissatisfaction on the job.

Patchen (1970) identified three general conditions for job involvement. According to him, "Where people are highly motivated, where they feel a sense of solidarity with the enterprise, and where they get a sense or pride for their work, we may speak of them as highly involved in their job".

When Patchen (1970) talks of workers being highly motivated, he refers to their high levels of achievements need or to their wish to accomplish worthwhile things on the job. When he talks of workers solidarity with the enterprise, he refers to their need for belonging to the organization. Finally, when he talks of worker's sense of pride, he refers to workers 'feeling of high self-esteem'. Thus in Patchen's view, when a job provides opportunities for the satisfaction on one's achievement needs, belonging needs and self-esteem needs, one experiences a greater degree of job involvement.

Researchers who are in favour of defining job involvement as a central component of self-image consider job involvement to be caused by early socialization on the individual. However, they still maintain that intrinsic need satisfaction is an important precondition for job involvement.

Lawler and Hall (1970) are also in favour of defining job involvement as the psychological identification with the work. They believe that job involvement is partly caused by an individual's personal background and situations.

The above review of the causes of job involvement shows that almost all researchers consider intrinsic need satisfaction as the necessary condition for job involvement. The satisfaction of intrinsic needs of workers can be achieved only through appropriate changes in the job and the organizational environment.

Such changes like job variety, autonomy, opportunity for participation have also been viewed as situational factors causing job involvement. Besides the situational variables at the workplace that affect intrinsic motivation, researchers have also identified the protestant–work–ethic attitude as a cause of job involvement.

The protestant–work–ethic attitude is largely determined by post-socialisation processes experienced by individuals in specific socio-economic and cultural milieu in which they live. Thus, the rural/urban, blue collar / white collar and ethno-cultural backgrounds of individuals have been considered as causes of job involvement. Thus, Roibinwitz and Hall (1977) consider the protestant–work–ethic attitude as a personal factor or individual–difference variable causing job involvement.

JOB CHARACTERISTICS vs JOB INVOLVEMENT

It is important to know what characteristics of the job are related to job involvement. Herzberg (1966) has divided job characteristics into two groups i.e. job content factors and job context factors. Although job involvement can be related to changes in both sets of factors, most psychological researchers have advocated changes only in the job content factors. Herzberg proposed job-enrichment programmes as a means to increase job involvement, based on the belief that job involvement results from those job changes that satisfy workers' intrinsic needs.

Hackman and Oldharm (1976) identified five core job characteristics (Variety, autonomy, task identify, task significance and feedback) that need to be introduced in a job-enrichment programme.

Tannenbaum (1966) argued that workers holding higher–level jobs in an organization should show more job involvement than workers holding lower-level jobs.

This expectation is based on the assumption that higher-level jobs can satisfy intrinsic needs to a greater extent by offering more variety, autonomy and challenge to the workers than the lower-level jobs. However, studies performed on this issue provided mixed results.

IMPORTANCE OF THE STUDY

There seems to be a growing discontentment on the part of the Teacher Educators towards their job as a result of which standards of education are falling. Is it a fact that the teachers are really dissatisfied in spite of the different plans and programmes which have been implemented to improve their lot?

Studies on job satisfaction seem to have begun with the famous Hawthorne studies conducted by Elton Mayo at the Western Electric company in the 1920s. Most of the studies conducted so far are in industrial setting and examining the effects of physical conditions design of equipment etc., on job satisfaction and productivity. Elton Mayo and his co-workers started very much in this direction. During the course of their investigations, however they became convinced that factors of a social nature also affect job satisfaction and productivity. The human relations school was thus born, which saw the function of the industrial psychologist as seeking to improve the happiness of the worker, and through this to improve productivity. The implicit assumption, of course, was that the satisfied worker produced more.

The traditional model of job satisfaction is that it consists of the total body of feelings about the nature of the job. If the sum total of influence of these factors given rise to feelings of satisfaction, the individual is satisfied. Changing any one of these influences will lead in the direction of job satisfaction or dissatisfaction depending upon the nature of the change.

Locke (1969) however emphasises the concept of value fulfillment rather than expectation satisfactions occurs when the job fulfills what one values just as expectations values vary from group to group and between individuals with in the group.

The colleges of education in Andhra Pradesh are controlled by two types of managements—government and private. With the impact of privatisation and the reservation policy of the government the minority and non-minority institutions are also there in this state.

Has the type of management under which the teachers work any effect on the job satisfaction of teachers? Very often it is felt that teachers in government colleges will be more satisfied with their jobs than that of teacher's working under private managements. But investigations by Venkata Rami

Reddy and Krishna Reddy (1978); Venkata Rami Reddy and Babjan (1980) and Venkata Rami Reddy and Ramakrishnaiah (1981) showed that teachers in private institutions were more satisfied with their job than that those in government colleges.

Similarly, is there any significant difference between the job satisfaction of men and women teachers? What are the other correlates of job satisfaction? Is it related to attitude towards teaching? Not much is known about these as very few empirical studies have been carried out, especially on Indian samples. Investigation into these factors may throw light on many aspects of job satisfaction.

The progress and standard of job of any nation cannot be beyond the standard of her system of education and the standard of her educational institutions. The standard of any educational institutions in turn, cannot rise beyond the levels of its teachers. It commissions that high quality personnel, who have the necessary aptitude for teaching and favorable attitude towards teaching should be selected for the teaching profession. Further, it is believed that certain personality traits are desirable for the teaching profession. It would be rewarding, therefore, to identify the type of attitude and personality characteristics that are conducive for driving satisfaction in the teaching profession. This knowledge may help in selecting the best suited to the teaching profession.

CONCLUSION

Can we really play the role of such illuminated lamps? Are the present Teacher Educators, available in our Teacher Education institutions, capable of providing the needed quality Teacher Education? Here an attempt is made to seek answer to these questions in the contest of the competence of our teacher educators working in B.Ed. colleges along with the existing conditions and practices available for educating them as Teacher Educators.

Teacher Educators have a key role in improvement of Education. Therefore, it is important that their best efforts be devoted to it. Since there is so much flexibility in the work they are required to do, and the manner in which they can do it, the contribution they make to the field depend on part of their involvement in their work and the satisfactions they derive from it. Hence, the investigator is interested to know the satisfaction of Teacher Educators working in B.Ed. colleges with respect of different variables.

Thus, the present study 'Job Satisfaction of Teacher Educators working in B.Ed. Colleges" is designed to analyse the job satisfaction of the Teacher Educators in relation to different variables like management, sex, teaching experience, salary, involvement, personality traits and self-concepts etc.

CHAPTER 2

REVIEW OF RELATED LITERATURE

This chapter deals with the internal review of the literature. It is an attempt to discover relevant material published about the problem under study. This covers the empirical research study done previously in the problem area.

IMPORTANCE OF THE REVIEW

Review of literature gives us the revelant material published in the problem area under study. The studies conducted during the last few decades in the field of the Teacher Education that are more revelant and pertaining to the present investigation are discussed in this chapter.

The literature provides ideas, theories explanation etc., valuable in formulating the problems and methods of research appropriate to it. The advantage of knowledge which has accumulated in the past, is a result of human endeavour. A careful review of the research journals, books, dissertations and other sources of information on the problems to be investigated are one of the important steps in planning of any research work. In other words, research work begins in vacuum. The related literature is worthwhile for an effective research.

In the field of education as in the other fields too, the research worker needs to acquire up-to-date information about what has been thought and done in the particular area from which the investigator intends to take up a problem for research. But it is found that generally the extent of important, up-to-date information regarding educational research and ideas possessed by educational workers is very limited.

Study of the related literature allows the researcher to acquaint himself with current knowledge in the field or area in which he is going to conduct research serves the following purposes:

- The study of related literature enables the researcher to define the limits of his/her field.
- The researcher can select those areas in which positive findings are very likely to result and his/her endeavours would be likely to add to the knowledge in a meaningful way.
- It gives the researcher an understanding of the research methodology, which refers to the way the study is to be conducted.
- It locates comparative data and findings useful in the interpretation and discussion of results.
- It helps in developing expertise and general scholarship of the investigator in the area investigated.

Keeping in view these purposes the investigator makes a study of the related literature in the following pages.

NEED TO KNOW ABOUT THE RELATED LITERATURE

According to Best (1959) "Practically all human knowledge can be found in books and libraries. Unlike other animals that must start a new with each generation, man builds upon accumulated and recorded knowledge of the past". Review of related literature widens knowledge, deepens understanding and builds up ideas and insights for better perspective and therefore is an essential aspect of research. The availability and utilization of adequate sources of related information are essential for a proper research activity. It gives adequate information about different researches related to the present study. It also guides and directs the researcher to collect useful material for the purpose of study.

Availability of adequate information about educational thought and research does not by itself result in possession of its knowledge by the investigator. The investigator may be very keen to possess up–to-date information regarding his field, and may try hard to be posted up-to-date, and yet fail to get enough information due to the non-assistance of sources are such information.

Survey of related literature besides forming one of the early chapters in research report for orienting the researcher, surveys have some other purposes.

Good, Barr and Scates (1941) analysed these purposes as given under:

- To show whether the available evidence material solves the problem adequately without further investigation.
- To provide ideas, theories, explanations or hypotheses valuable in formulating the present study.
- To suggest the research methods to the problem.
- To locate comparative data useful in the interpretation of the results.
- To contribute the general scholarship of the investigator.

MEANING OF JOB SATISFACTION

Man in any working situation is able to apply himself whole-heartedly to his work when he enjoys job satisfaction. This is possible only when he has adjusted himself well to his job and other related factors. Cilmer (1966) defined job satisfaction or dissatisfaction as "the result of various attitudes the person held towards his job, towards related factors and towards life in general." A more comprehensive approach to the physical, social, temperamental and personality factors be included for correct assessment (Blum, 1956). Job satisfaction is a complex phenomenon, as described by Rao (1970), having multiple inter-correlated causal factors: personal, social, cultural and economic. Again Blum and Naylor (1968) believe that job satisfaction is the result of the various attitudes possessed by the employee which relate to the job and are concerned with several specific job aspects.

Job: According to Good (1973), job is,

- A test performed by a student in order to develop skill or to "try out" the application of a principle.
- A unit of trade or task done by a worker in return for pays, an employment classification.
- A contract or unit of work in the Dalton Plan to be completed in a given time.
- A specific assigned tasks, which provides the media by which the student practices and develops skills for an occupation.

Satisfaction

The term satisfaction has been defined by English (1934) as "the state of a person whose tendencies have (for the moment, at least) reached their goal." In other words the term is defined as "affective condition of a person who gained his desires." This definition of the term satisfaction leads, altogether a theory which will be discussed later. In support of the above definition Blum (1956) defined job satisfaction as 'a complex of employee's attitudes. When there is a conflict between opposing drives, needs and desires in the vocational area, it leads to job dissatisfaction. In other words job satisfaction is the employee's judgement of how well his job, on the whole, satisfies his various needs.

Job Satisfaction

Job satisfaction is generally defined as affective responses to discriminate characteristics or facets of the task and work environment. These affective responses vary along a like/dislike continuum and reflect a complex process of comparisons between what is experienced on the job, frames of reference which workers have for evaluating what they experience, their expectations regarding what is a fair and equitable return for their efforts; and alternatives available to workers. In agreement with this, Wolman (1977) defines job satisfaction as "workers satisfactions with different characteristics of their jobs are considered specific instances of the more general class of affective responses labled attitudes."

Employees expect some rewards by doing their work. If the job in which they are involved will not provide their expected rewards, then they will be dissatisfied. Porter and Lawler (1967) concluded that an individual's satisfaction was a function both of the magnitude and the frequency of rewards he would receive as well as his expected equitable rewards. This model predicts low but positive relationship between job satisfaction and performance because of the imperfect relationship between performance, rewards and satisfaction. A similar type of definition has been given by Smith, et.al.,(1969). According to them "Job satisfaction represents the difference between 'what is expected' and 'what is experienced', in relation to the alternativc available in a given situation." This difference is termed as job discrimination index, which is intended to measure the affective responses to this difference by measuring feelings associated with different facets of the job satisfaction. Porter and Lawler (1967) described job satisfaction as a function of "the extent to which rewards actually received meet or exceed the perceived equitable level of rewards". The greater the failure of 'rewards actually received' to meet the 'perceived equitable level of rewards' the greater is the dissatisfaction.

It is suggested that the attitudes and motivations of a worker are influenced both by his self-image and his career situation. According to Crites (1961)... "if it is some specific aspect of the job such as duties and tasks or working conditions the concept which is defined, would be job attitudes. If it is the overall job in which the individual is presently employed, then the concept would be job satisfaction.....". And if the referent includes the work group and/or employing organization as well as job or vocational satisfaction, the concept would be morale" similarly, Blum (1956) clarified the confusion in the terminology as follows. He made the point that 'employee attitude', 'Job satisfaction' and 'industrial morale' were not synonymous. An attitude might contribute to job satisfaction, since the latter was comprised of a number of attitudes. Similarly, job satisfaction was not the same as industrial morale, although it might contribute to morale.

Pestonjee and Smith (1973), defined job satisfaction in the light of Herzberg's two factor theory and concluded that job satisfaction can be taken as a summation of employee's feelings in four important areas. Two of these (job and management) encompass factors directly concerned with the job (intrinsic factors) and the remaining two (social relations and personal adjustment) include factors not directly connected with the job (extrinsic factors) but which are presumed to have a bearing on job satisfaction. Sinha and Agarwal (1971) defined job satisfaction as "a persistent effective state which has arisen in the individual as a function of the perceived characteristics of his job in relation to his frame of reference.

Thus, there are numerous definitions and meanings for the concept of job satisfaction. To conclude, different operational definitions of job satisfaction given by Wanous and Lawler (1972) may be quoted.

1. "Overall job satisfaction is the sum of job facet satisfaction across all facets of a job".
2. "Job satisfaction has been conceptualized as a weighted sum of job facet satisfaction."
3. "Job satisfaction has been operationalised as the sum of goal attainment or need fulfillment when summed across job facets."

4. "Job satisfaction has been operationlised as a discrepancy between 'how much is there now' and 'how much should there be".

Theories on Job Satisfaction

Several theories exist concerning the dynamics of job satisfaction and its general impact upon worker behaviour. A brief mention of prominent of these seems appropriate. Brophy (1959) classified theories of job satisfaction into four types—need, explanation, role and self.

The Need Theory was proposed by Morse (1953). According to this, a worker's satisfaction depends upon the function of two factors: 'how much his needs are fulfillment by being in a particular situation' and 'how much his needs remain unfulfillment'. Thus, for calculating the amount of satisfaction the following equation may be used:

$S=f(T_1-T_2)$, where 'S' is satisfaction,

'T_1' is worker's initial tension level,

'T_2' is the tension level after exposed to the vocation.

The Explanation Theory is based upon the hypothesis is that an individual's degree of satisfaction with an activity leading towards a goal is an inverse function of the level of his perceived probability of attaining the goal both in a situation when the goal is attained and in a situation when it is not attained. Katzell's (1964) theory is also based on this model.

The characteristics of the sociological Role Theory are (1) it involves an evaluation of the environment from a view-point external to the individual's rather than from his own phenomenological frame of reference; (2) it considers an aggregate of the individual positions as a single position, and (3) it focuses on people, rather than upon a single person and his interaction with the environment.

According to the Self Theory, vocational satisfaction is a function of agreement among the worker's self-concept, both real and ideal, and the occupational roles he perceives or plays in the world of work.

(a) Need Satisfaction Theory (Maslow's Hierarchy of Needs)

Apart from the above classification of theories of job satisfaction, there are few more individual theories, of course, with a little bit overlap from the above mentioned theories. Maslow (1943) has proposed an interesting theory concerning human needs and their effect upon human behaviour. He suggests that human needs may be classified into five different groups as (1) Physio-psychological needs, (2) Safety needs, (3) love needs, (4) Esteem needs, and (5) Self-actualization needs.

His basic premises are that (1) the behaviour of any person is dominated and determined by the most basic groups of needs which are unfulfilled; (2) the individual will systematically satisfy his needs, starting with the most basic and moving up the hierarchy; and (3) more basic needs groups are said to be proponent in that they will take precedent over all those higher in the hierarchy.

Maslow enumerated five needs which he arranged in a rank order. The extent to which the total job environment or the various segments of the job environment contribute to the satisfaction of these needs determines the job satisfaction of workers.

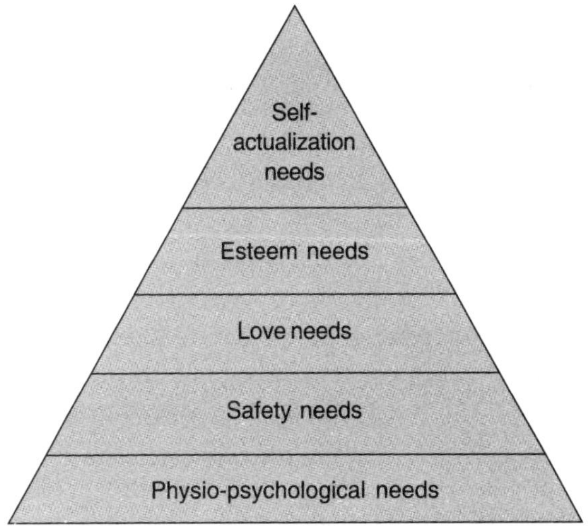

Fig. 2.1. Maslow's Hierarchy of Needs

Following this theory of job satisfaction, many psychologists and researchers in the field of personnel management have proposed slightly varied hypothesis that overall satisfaction will vary directly with the extent to which those needs of an individual which can be satisfied in a job are actually satisfied, the stronger the need, the more closely will job satisfaction depend on its fulfillment. Similarly Pestonjee (1973) observed that the job satisfaction is generated by the individual's perception of how well his job, on the whole, is satisfying his various needs.

Porter (1961) developed a questionnaire containing 15 items designed to provide information about five different motivational need classes which were derived from Maslow. Porter defined need fulfillment as the difference between 'how much there should be' and 'how much is now' connected with each of the fifteen items. Blai (1982) hypothesized that, in the work environment, degrees of self-assessed job satisfactions vary with the strength of the psychological needs satisfied.

(b) Two Factor Theory

Herzberg, Mausner and Snyderman (1959) proposed a model of job satisfaction called Two Factor Theory. No theory of job satisfaction has received as much attention or has been subjected to as much criticism as has this model. The original study was concerned with an investigation into the causes of job satisfaction and dissatisfaction. Each worker was asked to describe, in detail, times when he felt exceptionally 'good' or exceptionally 'bad' about his job. The responses were then content analysed. Thus, the theory was derived from research using semi-structured, critical incident interviews. The results of their study did indicate that things which were associated with the high satisfaction (satisfiers) were some what different from the things which were associated with the situations of low satisfaction (dissatisfies). They found that the descriptions of good periods included such things as achievement, recognition, advancement, responsibility, etc. All of these things seemed to relate to the actual content of the job and therefore, they were called 'intrinsic' or 'content' factors or motivators. Descriptions of bad work periods seemed to be filled with items dealing with company policy, supervision, salary, and working conditions. These items seemed to relate to the context in which a person performed his task and were, therefore, referred to as 'intrinsic' or 'context' or 'hygiene' factors. Because the model postulates two general classes of variables—one class which can satisfy but not dissatisfy and one which causes dissatisfaction but not satisfaction—the model has been designated as 'Herzberg's Two Factor Theory'.

Studies using this technique consistently yielded results in which motivators were cited primarily as sources of satisfaction and hygienes primarily as sources of dissatisfaction (Herzberg, 1966) and provided the primary evidence in support of the theory. Holdaway (1978) found a substantial positive relationships between overall satisfaction and achievement, career orientation, recognition, and stimulation. These latter variables were described by Herzberg as 'motivators'. Facets receiving the highest percentages 'satisfied' mainly involved inter-personal relationships, and freedom in the teaching assignment. Facets receiving the highest percentages 'dissatisfied' mainly involved social and parental attitudes, preparation time and decision-making procedures. Myers (1964) found that satisfaction was related to intrinsic work factors and dissatisfaction to extrinsic factors. Similar results were obtained by Schwartz, Jenusaitis and Stark (1963) in favour of the two factor theory.

Blum and Naylor (1968) while reviewing the literature, pointed out that the factors involved in feelings of satisfaction and dissatisfaction do not appear to divide as neatly as assumed by Herzberg's original studies. Ewen *et. al.,* (1966) tested a number of hypotheses by using the data provided by 793 employees from various jobs. They found that the results supported neither the Herzberg's two factor theory nor the traditional theory. Instead, results indicated that intrinsic factors were more strongly related to both overall satisfaction and overall dissatisfaction than the extrinsic factors. Armstrong (1971) also concluded that the Herzberg's dichotomy was not supported. Sarveswara Rao (1972) found that both motivators and hygiene's contributed to satisfaction and also to dissatisfaction. Limited support for the hypotheses that the dimensional independence of satisfaction and dissatisfaction was found and hence the assumption underlying the 2-factors theory was questioned. Locke and Whiting (1974) also tested Herzberg's two factor theory and concluded that it was not supported.

(c) Valence Theory of Job Satisfaction

Vroom (1964) proposed a theory of human motivation which took as its context the individual in the world of work. He used the basic concept of 'valence' as a key notion. He defined valence as "the attractiveness of a goal or outcome." Another definition was "the anticipated satisfaction from an outcome." Vroom suggested that job satisfaction was a reflection of how desirable a person found his job—thus, it was a measure of a person's valence for his work situation. His model predicted the direct relationship between the valence of his job and turnover and absentceism. Vroom equated job satisfaction with the valence of the job or work role. The overall valence of work role is useful in predicting behaviour in relation to the total work role.

(d) Other Theories

The other theories of job satisfaction are not so popular as the above theories. But a few researches were undertaken applying these theories. They are very briefly described one by one. Scott (1966) suggested that 'activation theory' was a very appropriate model for understanding the behaviour in work environment. Briefly, activation theory states that the human organism needs stimulation and variety in its environment, without this, motivation will suffer and frustration may result. Smith, Kendall and Hulin (1969) defined job satisfaction as feelings of affective responses to the work situation. In addition, they posited that these responses are best explained by a discrepancy between the work motivation attitudes and the incentives offered by the organizations. Similar conceptualizations are the inducement-contributions theory (March and Siman, 1958), the cognitive dissonance theory (Festinger, 1957) and the inequity theory (Adams, 1963). The basic postulate of these positions is that job satisfaction levels are related to the perceived difference between what is expected or desired as a fair and reasonable return (individual motivation) and what is actually experienced in the job situation (organizational incentives).

Level of Dissatisfaction

The per cent of dissatisfaction among workers in different professions at various cadres vary because of many reasons. The factors causing dissatisfaction may be different for different people in different jobs. Similarly the level of satisfaction/ dissatisfaction also vary from job to job. Hoppock (1935) reported that the job satisfaction varied almost from '0' to '100' per cent, depending on the job. In the study on early community wide survey in the town of New Hope, Hoppock (1935) found that 15 per cent of the sample had negative attitudes or job dissatisfaction. At another instance, he stated that the majority of the gainfully employed, tended to have job satisfaction or were at least neutral and only a small percentage had dissatisfied. When Hoppock (1935) reviewed 32 investigations, it was found that 2/3 of the studies showed less than 1/3 of the workers to be dissatisfied. Again in his study, when the subjects were invited to take their choice of all the jobs in the world, 36 per cent indicated that they would leave their present occupations. 66 per cent got more satisfaction from their jobs than from the things they did in their spare time.

The Fortune Quarterly Survey XI (1938) reported that 60 per cent of the factory workers were dissatisfied with their jobs, whereas only 30 per cent of the professionals were dissatisfied. Form (1946) reported that almost half of a group of clerks and manual workers stated that they were very happy with their occupations, but only 17 per cent said that they would like to enter their present occupation again. Robinson and Hoppock (1952) collected the data on 191 assorted studies reporting percentages of job dissatisfaction and found that the median figure of dissatisfied was 18 per cent. Similarly Herzberg *et al.,* (1957) from their review of 22 studies found that the average figure of job dissatisfaction in different industries was around 13 per cent.

Harrell (1958) reported that 95 per cent of a group of teachers expressed satisfaction with their job, whereas 98 per cent of a group of textile operatives expressed dissatisfaction with their jobs. Robinson (1959) estimated the median value of dissatisfied employees as approximately 13 per cent based upon the results of a large number of job satisfaction a studies spanning over many years. Blauner (1963) made the point that from many studies there was a remarkable consistency in the findings that the vast majority of people, virtually in all occupations and industries, were moderately or highly satisfied.

Parassiva Murthy (1966) studies 44 out of 176 employees in an organization and found that 43.18 per cent of the workers were satisfied and 4.55 per cent of them were dissatisfied with their job. Becavar (1969) found that elementary teachers experienced greater satisfaction than they anticipated in teaching while secondary teachers experienced less satisfaction level among the primary and secondary school teachers.

In a study by Marr and Mathur (1973) it was observed that the largest number of Teacher Educators were satisfied. Costello and Lee (1974) investigated the relationship between need fulfillment and job satisfaction among 164 professional employees and found that 80 per cent of the sample indicated an overall job satisfaction. Bernard and

Kulandaivel (1976) undertook a study to see how far the graduate teachers were satisfied with their job. The findings showed that in general the high school teachers were satisfied with their job. Only 8 per cent were extremely dissatisfied and 32 per cent were extremely satisfied. The middle 60 per cent of the sample of teachers were moderately satisfied.

Goble (1977) showed that a majority of workers, in a job satisfaction survey, on broiler processing plant, were dissatisfied with their work. Sheppard and Herrick (1972) reported that the dissatisfaction with dehumanizing aspects of technology was widespread nationwide among the white and blue-colour union members and youthful workers.

Benoit (1977) conducted a survey of job satisfaction among 220 faculty women in higher education (women working in state university of Lovisiana). The results on the Minnesota satisfaction Questionnaire indicated that the faculty women were less satisfied than other groups on whom the same questionnaire was administered.

Rajagopalan and Rajaraman (1977) conducted an enquiry on 200 teachers of postgraduate classes in Madras University and found that 66 per cent of teachers were not interested to quit their job even if they were offered any other job. The percentage was slightly higher among research degree holders. 27 per cent of teachers reacted that they would consider such offers and 5 per cent expressed that they would jump at a situations.

Gartner (1981), the author of the report of a survey conducted by National Educational Association, concluded that the dissatisfaction among teachers was increasing. He compared the results of the survey with the results obtained in the similar survey conducted 20 years ago and found that the percentage of teachers who would choose the teaching profession again was decreased from 80 per cent to 46 per cent and the percentage of teachers who would not choose the teaching profession again was increased from 11 per cent to 33 per cent within 20 years. Thus the dissatisfaction among the teachers increased. Maddux (1982) from a survey on Texas Public School teachers also found that 1/3 of the teachers were considering to leave the profession because they were dissatisfied.

Causes of Dissatisfaction or Satisfaction

From the above review it is observed that the per cent of dissatisfied workers in general and teachers in particular is increasing. The reasons for their dissatisfaction or satisfaction may be many. The review of past studies is necessary to identify the most common factors causing either satisfaction or dissatisfaction.

Hoppock (1935) explained a dissatisfied person as one who has indicated a distinct and conscious discontent with his job as a whole, according to certain criteria. Horzberg et. al., (1957) concluded after their review of research on job attitudes that 'sustained job-interest' was very much important for professional people. Sud (1972) observed that need for motivating workers arised because of the following reasons:

1. The employee's usual remuneration (pay or salary) might be insufficient for his paramount needs.
2. The remuneration might be in commensurate with the work effort required from the employee.
3. The employee might be expected to perform his tasks in a way which prevented him from deriving adequate satisfaction from other activities.

National Education Association (1981) found "teachers today have more education and experience than they did five years ago, but they consider themselves underpaid and are less sure that they have chosen teaching as a profession if they have the chance to choose again." Gartner (1981), the author have the report, further clarified that teachers were quite dissatisfied with a number of things: salaries, stress, the amount of positive reinforcement they receive from parents, their self-concept, etc. Porter (1962) reported that all the respondents felt that there should be more opportunity for their different needs to be fulfilled than actually existed. Sheppard and Herick (1972) reported that the reason for widespread dissatisfaction among nationwide sample of workers was dehumanizing aspects of technology.

Colstello and Lee (1974) found that most subjects were satisfied with their social and security needs and their greatest deficiency was among higher order needs. It was concluded that management should provide incentives to satisfy self-esteem, autonomy and self-actualization needs in order to motivate professional employees. In a study by Marr and Mathur (1973) it was observed that the large number of Teacher Educators found their work interesting and hence they were satisfied. Converdale (1973) reported high dissatisfaction among teachers due to bad conditions of service, namely, the inspectorial and transfer system, promotion structure, status, class size, demands on teachers and curriculum, rather than material benefits.

Becvar (1969) found that elementary teachers experienced much satisfaction with the opportunity to be busy in teaching. On the other hand Kalanidhi (1973) concluded that those with personal, financial and /or family strain had less job satisfaction or were more dissatisfied than others without any strain. The factors contributing to satisfaction were moral values, social service and activity, and the factors contributing to dissatisfaction were university policies and practices, advancement and compensation (Benoit, 1977). Rajagopalan and Rajaraman (1977) also concluded that the factors for postgraduate teachers' unhappiness were their management and unsatisfactory student composition.

Studies on Job Satisfaction

Studies of community college instructors' job satisfaction have been conducted since the early 1900s, using a variety of theoretical constructs and measuring widely different dimensions of satisfaction. One group of studies has looked at the effects of personality variables and personal characteristics on job satisfaction, while another group has investigated working conditions and specific work activities as causes of teacher burnout and job dissatisfaction. In his review of five national and regional studies of job satisfaction, Friedlander (1963) concludes that measures of general job satisfaction are more accurate predictors of faculty members' desire to remain at their job than measures of attitudes toward working conditions.

Hoppock (1935) conducted a survey on people in the teaching profession. Five hundred teachers from 51 urban and rural communities in the north-eastern United States, estimated their job satisfaction on four attitude scales. Of this group, the 100 most satisfied and 100 least satisfied were asked about 200 questions. A comparison of their answers differentiated the satisfied from the dissatisfied teachers in the following areas:

1. The satisfied showed fewer indications of emotional maladjustments.
2. The satisfied were more religious.
3. The satisfied are enjoyed better human relationships with their superiors and associates.
4. The satisfied were teaching in the cities of over 10,000 populations.
5. The satisfied felt more successful.
6. Family influence and social status were more among the satisfied.
7. The satisfied 'selected' their vocations.
8. Monotony and fatigue were reported more frequently by the dissatisfied.
9. The satisfied averaged 7.5 years older.

Weitz and Nuckolos (1955) found that the decision to accept a new job would depend on anticipations of value fulfillments. To the extent that the expectations failed to materialise, job satisfaction would be relatively low and the likelihood of quitting the job would be relatively great.

The job satisfaction research literature has been thoroughly reviewed at intervals of about a decade in the past half century. Brayfield and Crockett (1955), Vroom (1964), and Locke (1974) each summarized the field extensively and observed the limited influence of satisfaction on work output. There is a need to study this aspect again in the present day context. The range-of-affect hypothesis (Locke, 1974) argues that facet importance is a key determinant of the level of satisfaction associated with any particular job facet. A larger range of facet satisfaction is expected for workers placing greater personal importance on a job facet (i.e., greater satisfaction with favorable conditions and greater dissatisfaction with unfavorable conditions).

Herzberg (1957) pointed out that for people at higher occupational and /or educational levels, intrinsic aspects of the job go up in importance, while security drops off considerably. This is no doubt due to the greater 'marketability' possessed by the people in the higher occupational strata.

Crites (1961) analysed three relatively new measures of work motives and values and identified the following five orthogonal factors: material security *vs.* job freedom; personal status *vs.* social service; social approach; system; and structure.

According to Blum (1961), a person might select a job where elements of security and other hygiene factors are high. Other persons, less concerned with security, choose jobs in which motivators or satisfiers are high. Williams (1965) findings that low risk takers are more concerned with intrinsic characteristics support Blum's (1961) conclusions.

Halpern (1966) on 93 subjects matched for equal satisfaction on motivator and hygiene aspects of their jobs, it was found that the work itself and opportunity for advancement accounted for nearly all the variance in overall job satisfaction.

Hackman and Lawler (1971) found that when jobs are high on the four core dimensions (variety, autonomy, task identity, and feedback), employees who are desirous of higher order need satisfaction (obtaining feelings of accomplishment, personal growth) tend to be treated by supervisors as doing high quality work.

After 1973, as job satisfaction research mutated into the Quality of Work Life movement, concern among serious scientists with job satisfaction as a major research paradigm faded.

Schmidt (1976) pointed out the importance of motivational factors like achievement, recognition, advancement, responsibility of work itself for job satisfaction.

According to Hackman and Oldham (1976) a job high in potential will not affect all individuals in the same way, particularly people who strongly value and desire personal accomplishment and growth, would respond very positive to a job which is high on the core dimensions; individuals who do not value personal growth and accomplishment may find such a job anxiety-arousing and may be uncomfortably 'stretched' by it.

From a motivational point of view, Sergiovanni (1975) suggested that over the long haul external standards and impersonal control mechanisms unduly programme teacher activity and behaviour and reduce the amount of discretion at the teaching level and also lower the amount of influence which teachers and students have over classroom activity.

According to Schmidt (1976) administrators are highly motivated by achievement, recognition and advancement in their profession.

Robert's (1977) study indicated that teachers ranked challenging work, good interpersonal relations, achievement of objectives, good wages, and fair and competent supervision as the most important of the thirteen job motivation factors.

Two important sources of job satisfaction have been suggested by Fares (1977). The motivator factors commonly associated with meaningful work experiences appeared to provide an intrinsic source of job satisfaction. In addition to this, perceived success attained through achievement on the job and advancement through the organizational hierarchy, appeared to be major determinants of job satisfaction.

According to Davis (1981), the primary sources of satisfaction of teachers were in aspects of working with students, intellectual stimulation, autonomy, holidays, and job security. Teacher satisfaction according to Daly (1981) is affected primarily by objective feedback or individual perception as to the prevailing performance level of the school.

Karugu's (1981) study indicated that the Kenyan educators in the sample groups identified job security, sense of building the nation, chance to continue learning, love of jobs itself (Noble), love for children, extracurricular activities, and communication with teachers, parents, and pupils as the most satisfying job factors in their current positions and also as the factors which cause them to retain their positions.

As per Gordon (1981) Teachers as a total group, indicated that they were most satisfied in the following areas: social service, creativity, moral values, and responsibility.

Kuhn (1982) found that satisfied teachers are centered on intrinsic aspects of work, predominantly, helping students. It was found that satisfaction was a result of an achievement on the job, interpersonal relations and recognition; and satisfaction was likely to result in feelings of increased job commitment.

The most important job dimensions motivating employees were work itself, achievement, relationship with peers, working conditions and relationship with supervisors (Al-Khaldi, 1983).

Review of organizational behavior for the Annual Review of Psychology, Barry Staw (1984) dismissed attitude surveys and satisfaction measures as "throw-away variables," characterizing the field as dominantly correlational in method and "rather a theoretical."

Ahmed (1984) found that the most important predictors for teachers' feelings of job satisfaction were the amount of pay offered by the job, the degree of help received from superiors, and the amount of say teachers had in decision-making. Least important predictors for job satisfaction were found to be opportunity for promotion and the degree of fairness of workload.

Satisfaction influences how individuals describe their jobs. Satisfied individuals may see their jobs as more 'complex' than dissatisfied individuals (Loher, et. a1., 1985).

Birmingham (1985) found that teachers were most satisfied with intrinsic reinforces such as social service, creativity, variety and ability utilization.

Iaffaldano and Muchinsky (1985) updated the job satisfaction literature. They confirmed the limited causal relationship between worker satisfaction and work output, lamenting that "empirical support for the satisfaction-performance relation does not approximate the degree to which this relation has been exposed in theories of organizational design." With so much disconfirmation, it would seem that the presumed relation of job satisfaction and work performance should long ago have been left behind as a dead-end issue.

Ramakrishnaiah (1990) in a study of job satisfaction of college teachers concluded that the factors: head of the institution, physical facilities, self-esteem, fringe benefits, entertainment, prestige, academic policies and co-teachers had played a significant role in uplifting the job satisfaction.

Malole (1993) observed that "Responsibility, interpersonal relations with students achievement, interpersonal relations with other teachers and job security to be the primary contributes to the job satisfaction.

Satisfied teachers expected to hold their jobs longer, to be able to engage in more responsive, positive and consistent interaction with children, and to influence positively students' performance (Maslach and Leiter, 1999). Thus, it is easy to understand why burnout and job satisfaction among teachers continues to be an enduring research issue. According to Lease (1998) job satisfaction can be viewed as the degree of an employee's affective orientation toward the work-role occupied in the organization. Research on teachers' job satisfaction and the orientation toward the work-role occupied in the organisation is positive. Research on teachers' job satisfaction suggests that educators are most satisfied from the teaching itself and their supervision and dissatisfied from their salary and promotional opportunities (Dinham and Scott, 2000; Koustelios, 2001; Oshagbemi, 1999). These findings seem to be robust across several different countries and cultural contexts (Koustelios, 2001).

Fenech (2006) reported poor work conditions, low salaries, heavy workloads, unrealistic expectations from managers, low professional status, organizational conflict, and reduced autonomy.

Usmani, S N et. al., (2006) revealed that teachers job satisfaction in relation to their personality type and type of school. In this study an attempt is made to investigate the level of job satisfaction among Sr. Sec. School Teachers in relation to their personality type (Type-A, Type-B and Type-AB) and the type of school. The study was carried out on a sample of 450 subjects. The data were collected though ABBPS (AB Behaviour Pattern Scale) and TJSQ (Teachers job satisfaction questionnaire). The t-ratio was calculated to find out the significance of difference between the sample means. The results reveal that there exists no significant difference in the level of job satisfaction among teachers of personality type A, B and AB and also between the teachers of Government and Government-aided schools. It was found that there exists significant difference in the level of job satisfaction of teachers of government and private schools and between Government-aided and unaided or private schools.

(i) Sex and Job Satisfaction

Many investigators considered 'sex' as one of the variables which would contribute to job satisfaction or dissatisfaction.

Bange (1944) and Stockford and Kunze (1950) found that women workers were more satisfied than men. Morse (1953) observed that a higher overall level of job satisfaction has been reported in various studies for women than for men. According to his work a less consuming element in the lives of women and hence of somewhat lesser importance to their status in the community.

Hollen and Gemmill (1976) reported that women teaching professionals experienced less perceived participation in decision making, less overall job satisfaction, and more job related tension than their men counterparts.

Studies on elementary and secondary school teachers (Chase, 1951; and Belesco and Alutto, 1972) have reported that women teachers tended to be more satisfied with their job than men teachers. Bernard and Kulandivel (1976) also found that women teachers expressed greater job satisfaction compared to their men counterparts.

Englhardt (1973) and Weaver (1977) however, did not find any significant difference between men and women workers with regard to their job satisfaction. Cohen's (1977) study also showed that men and women teachers are remarkably similar, sex was found to be unrelated to organizational affiliation, job consciousness, degree of participation in the local association and degree of participation in the job actions. Similarly, Atteberry (1977) reported no significant relationship between sex and job satisfaction of elementary school principals.

Gobel (1977) also found that women workers evidenced more dissatisfaction with work than did their men counterparts but they expressed more satisfaction with pay. Similarly, Chen (1977) observed that men teachers were more satisfied with their jobs than women teachers.

In a study on 240 secondary school teachers, Venkatarami Reddy and Krishna Reddy (1978) found that women teachers were more satisfied than men teachers. Venkatarami Reddy and Babjan (1980); and Venkatarami Reddy and Ramakrishnaiah (1981), Padmanabhaiah (1984) also obtained similar results.

Female teachers tend to be more satisfied with their current teaching profession and they perceive a more favourable professional environment than male teachers (Smith, 1982). Lewis (1982) and Birmingham (1985) also found that women teachers were more satisfied with their job than men teachers.

Among the university professors it was found that either no significant sex differences in job satisfaction exist or that, if found, the differences are not psychologically meaningful (Smith and Lewis, 1982). Surbida (1984) found that there was no significant relationship between principals' sex and their ratings of their overall job satisfaction.

Fumham and Goddard (1986) reported no gender difference in overall job satisfaction, although women were generally more satisfied with their working conditions than the men.

Pratap and Gupta (1986), in a study of 25 male and 25 female employees of similar age, some number of deponents and education working various banks found that females were more satisfied with their jobs than males.

Jalaja (2004) on the job satisfaction of the Teacher Educators found that there is no significant relationship between Teacher Educators sex and job satisfaction.

Srenivasan (2007) found that all the Teachers irrespect of sex were satisfied with their jobs.

(ii) Age and Job Satisfaction

Age of an individual is one of the most important demographic variable which influences job satisfaction.

There is widespread belief that productivity declines with age.

Hull and Kolstad (1942) observed the results of several investigations and concluded that job satisfaction was relatively high at the start, dropped slowly to the fifth or eighth year, then raised again with more time on the job. The highest morale was reached after the twentieth year.

Herzberg et. a1., (1957) in their review of research and opinion also reported that, in general job satisfaction was high among young workers, low among middle aged employees and it would increase again after the middle age.

Sinha and Sarma (1962), and Anand (1972) observed a significant relationship between age and job satisfaction. Altimus and Tersine (1973) found that younger workers were significantly better in satisfaction with work self-esteem, self-actualisation and total work satisfaction.

Saleh and Otis (1964) reported that job satisfaction increased up to 60 years of age and then declined in the terminal period of 60-65 years among the managers in different companies.

Age is also one of the most important variables in exercising its influence on job satisfaction. But the relationship between them is again complex as pointed by Hulin (1977) since it is confounded with job level, income, personal and family needs and expectations.

Belasco Ansl Alutto's (1972) study indicated that the most satisfied teachers to be older and teaching in the elementary school. Similar results were obtained by Smith (1982) and Al-Khaldi (1983). Birmingham (1985) also observed that teachers over 55 years of age and under 25 were the most-satisfied.

But three studies conducted by Rao (1970), Pestonjee and Singh (1973), Anand (1977) reported that there was no significant relationship between age and job satisfaction of workers. Surbida (1984) also observed that there was no significant relationship between principal's ages and their ratings of their overall job satisfaction.

Neeraja Dwivedi and Pestonjee (1975) also reported that age was the important factor which played a significant role in the determination of job satisfaction. Holdaway (1978) reported that both facet and overall satisfaction were related to age of the teacher. Kentle (1985) also found that age was significantly related to job satisfaction.

Richard and Dewhirst (1979) disclosed that age demonstrated a significant positive relationship with extrinsic satisfaction and there was no such relationship between age and intrinsic satisfaction.

Mokry (1981) in a study, found that the young female teachers begin their job with enthusiasm, hope and satisfaction and older female teachers end up with feeling of frustration, disappointment and dissatisfaction, whereas young male teachers begin their job with low or average feelings of satisfaction and end up with a somewhat better level of satisfaction.

Godkin (1982) also found a positive correlation between the age of respondents and the level of expected satisfaction on their job.

The study conducted by Rana (1990) too reported that there was no significant relationship between age and job satisfaction of workers. Das (1994) too observed that there was no significant relationship between principal's working in Degree College's ages and their ratings of their overall job satisfaction.

Surbida (1984) observed that there was no significant relationship between principal's age their ratings of their overall job satisfaction.

Kentle (1985) found that age was significantly related to job satisfaction.

Sajili (1995) reported that the satisfaction increased up to 45 years of age and then declined in the terminal period of 45-65 years among the lecturers in different institutions in Uttar Pradesh. Tripri's (1999) study revealed that the most satisfied teachers to be older and teaching in the middle school. Similar results were obtained by Shekah (2003). Aajana (2005) in her study observed that teachers over 55 years of age and under 25 were the most-satisfied.

Srenivasan (2007) observed that high age groups have more job satisfaction than low age groups.

(iii) Educational Qualification and Job Satisfaction

Educational qualifications brings changes in the job satisfaction and job involvement.

Happock (1935), Sinha and Sarma (1962), Anand (1972), Weaver (1974), and Bernard and Kulandaivel (1976) concluded that there was no relationship between level of education and job satisfaction among employees of various occupations.

Rao (1970) found that there was significant relationship between job satisfaction and education level of individuals. Carrell and Elbert (1974), in a study on postal clerks found that the educational qualification of the employees was one of the significant determinants of job satisfaction.

The teachers with Bachelor degrees were more satisfied with their work situation than those who had Master degrees, particularly in the areas of supervision and co-workers (Weiner, 1981).

Teachers with Master or higher degrees were more critical of the professional environment (Smith, 1982). Al-Khaldi (1983) found that employees with higher educational levels were less satisfied with their salary than those with lower education levels.

Anirudh and Mandal (1990) found that education had negative association with Job satisfaction.

Grau et al., (1991) investigated institutional loyalty and job satisfaction among nurse maids in nursing homes and found that the subjects with low education were significantly more satisfied with all dimensions of work except for social environment.

Shajan (1998) identified that teachers with Master or higher degrees were not satisfied with job than simple graduate.

Anjana (2000) too found that employees with higher educational levels were less satisfied with their salary than those with lower education levels.

Tanjoth (2004) found that there is no difference with teachers with Bachelor degrees and master's degree.

Srenivasan (2007) identified that postgraduates were satisfied with their job as compared with graduate teachers.

Work satisfaction is very much related with the qualifications in any area and there is a need to identify this factor among the Teacher Educators.

(iv) Teaching Experience and Job Satisfaction

According to Siegel (1969), job experience is related to satisfaction in a rather interesting fashion. As one might expect, new employees tend to be relatively well satisfied with their jobs.

Neeraja Dwivedi and Pestonjee (1975) found that job satisfaction increased with increasing experience for a period of 10 years and after that it starts going down. Hodge (1977) observed that the level of job satisfaction increased for both Negro and White Professors as years of employment at the institutions increase in number.

Weinroth (1977) indicated that experienced teachers, over 55 years of age, with older children, had lower motivation and higher job satisfaction in the intrinsic area compared to (1) the young, childless inexperienced teachers, and (2) older, experienced teachers with school aged children. Young inexperienced teachers with pre-school children wanted less work pressure and were less satisfied with the amount of pressure on the job than older, experienced teachers with school aged children. Lewis (1982) also found that teachers who had continuous experience in the current school were more satisfied than others.

But Rao (1970) found that there was no association between job satisfaction and experience. Anand (1977), Ramakrishnaiah (1980) and Padmanabhaiah (1984) in their studies pointed out that the years of experience possessed by teachers had no role to play in the determination of job satisfaction. No significant relationship existed between the number of years served as a principal and ratings of subjects and their overall job satisfaction (Surbida, 1984).

Srenivasan (2007) stated that low experience teachers have low job satisfaction than high experience teachers.

Neelakandan. and Rajendran (2007) indicated that high experience employees have higher job satisfaction than low experience employees. Gandharva and Joshi (1999) also agreed with this statement.

(v) Marital Status and Job Satisfaction

Neeraja Dwivedi and Pestonjee (1975) conducted a study on a group of 240 blue-collar workers who were working under a financial incentive scheme in a leading locomotive works and found that as far as marital status was concerned married workers showed higher job satisfaction than unmarried workers.

It was concluded by Weinroth (1977) that age, teaching experience, and age of children in the home affect the motivational needs, job satisfaction, and career aspirations of married women teachers.

Smith (1977) found that husband's marital adjustment was correlated with women's job satisfaction. Those who were generally happy and satisfied tended to reflect that feeling in both the major areas of their lives—work and family.

Generally, married adults are better adjusted than their unmarried counterparts (Srole, et a1., 1962; Orden and

Bradburn, 1968; Bradburn, 1969). As adjustment is positively related to job satisfaction (Kates, 1950; Herzberg et al., 1957; Anand, 1977; Balasubramanyam and Narayanan, 1977; Venkatarami Reddy and Krishna Reddy, 1978) one may expect that married teachers would be more satisfied with their jobs.

However, the few studies that were carried out in this area obtained contradictory results. AVA (1948), Redfer (1964), Venkatarami Reddy and Krishna Reddy (1978), Ramakrishnaiah (1980) and Padmanabhaiah (1984) reported no relationship between the two variables, while Butler (1961) found that unmarried beginning teachers were more satisfied than their married counterparts. However, Inlow (1951), NEA (1957) and Venkatarami Reddy and Babjan (1980) found that married teachers were more satisfied. Sinha and Nair (1965) and Chen (1977) also obtained similar results on factory workers.

Jalaja (2004) found again that married teachers seem to be more satisfied with their teaching positions than unmarried teachers.

Neelakandan and Rajendran (2007) found that married employees will have higher job satisfaction than compare to unmarried employees. The result is in agreement to finding of Bhatt (1999) and Bilgic Reyham (1998).

(vi) Salary and Job Satisfaction

Salary have an important influence on the satisfaction of the employees with increasing complexity and industrialization of society, for many people work is turning out, day by day, as a means of earning a living.

Anjaneyulu (1968) found that inadequate salary was one of the most common causes for dissatisfaction among school teachers.

Those who were working under financial incentives had better job satisfaction than those who were under no such incentives (Pestonjee, 1971). These findings laid support to

Ganguli's (1964) prediction that for the present and in the foreseeable future, money will remain as an important incentive for Indian workers.

It is very unfortunate that the scales of pay of teachers are lower than other categories of employees who possess similar or even lower qualifications, experience and responsibilities, observed Perumal (1969). He added that such a disparity promotes an unhealthy and undesirable competition and as a result, teachers become a disgusted and a dissatisfied lot.

According to Mishra (1972) in this age of materialism and run-away inflation, man's worth is judged by the size of his bank balance. Thus economic factors tend to overshadow all others. A radical improvement in the economic status will do much too attracted retain good teachers.

Neeraja Dwivedi and Pestonjee (1975) conducted a study on 'socio-personal correlates of job satisfaction' in which 240 blue-collar workers, who were working under a financial incentive scheme, were studied. The workers belonging to the high income group were found to be satisfied with their job. Income generally affected job satisfaction. However age and tenure of service were more effective correlates of job satisfaction than income and marital status.

In Robert's (1977) study, teachers ranked good wages as one of the most important job motivation factors. Similarly, Shaver (1977) observed that the biggest contribution among journalism graduates to job dissatisfaction was low salary.

In the same line, Schmidt (1976) concluded that salary was highly dissatisfying to the administrators when it was not effectively present.

According to Brown (1973) "An incentive is an objective goal which is capable of satisfying what we are aware of subjectively as a need, drive or desire". So monetary incentive or financial need or drive is one of the most and primary motives of work. Blum (1956) and Blum and Naylor (1968) states that in most of the studies financial incentives were found to be the most effective determinants of job satisfaction.

Counts (1978) conducted a study on public school teachers and found that inadequate salaries and the narrow salary range between beginning and retiring teachers were among the principal reasons for leaving the teaching profession.

Surbida (1984) indicated that overall, principals reported that they were satisfied with their jobs and their salaries. In Kentle's (1985) study income was rated highly important by 54 per cent of the respondents, however, only 33 per cent were satisfied with their income.

Uma's (1986) study noted that significant relationships existed between income and sense of competence and job satisfaction. Moore (1986) concluded that 83 per cent of teachers were satisfied with their work on daily basis. They were satisfied with every job facet except salary.

In a study conducted by Cobb (1986) on teachers indicated that elementary and secondary school teachers perceived basically the same level of job satisfaction when comparisons were made concerning the factor reports with principal, satisfaction with teaching, salary, workload and community pressures.

Sharma (2005) conducted a study of job satisfaction among the physical education teachers working in Himachal Pradesh schools found that majority of teachers satisfied with their salary.

(viii) Management and Job Satisfactions

Stagner, Flabee and Wood (1952) found that job satisfaction was related to better employee-employer relationship. When the behaviour of administrators conformed to teachers' expectations of the formers role, satisfaction was high; non-conformity produced high dissatisfaction (Bidwell, 1959).

Butler (1961) observed that degree of satisfaction was related to feeling of freedom or lack of it that was allowed by the management in the classroom.

Suehr (1962) found that communication was one of the most vital areas in the whole moral process. It was most conspicuous by its absence, and consequently intended to be a major source of dissatisfaction.

Anjaneyulu (1968) in his study on job satisfaction of secondary school teachers, educationists, inspecting officers, headmasters and retired teachers, found that in committee schools, the teachers were dissatisfied because of lack of job security, rigid and orthodox service conditions and too much of domination by the management. In mission schools, the factors were low standards of pupils, lack of parental co-operation and lack of right prospects in the job. In local board schools, the factors were too much interference by politicians, lack of social status, non-availability of suitable accommodation, equipment and furniture. In government schools, rigid and orthodox service conditions, lack of parental co-operation and frequent transfers to distant place were the factors, producing dissatisfaction.

Sommers (1969) also observed that most of the teachers felt that there was a lack of communication between teachers and administrators.

Bernard and Kulandaivel (1976) studied job satisfaction of high school teachers working under different managements and found that the teachers of aided schools appeared to be better satisfied than the teachers from municipal and government schools. It was also found the teachers working under different managements had different problems.

Smith (1977) found the satisfying elements in the principalship to be directly controlled by the principals themselves while control of the dissatisfying elements rested with the upper level school district management.

Venkatarami Reddy and Krishan Reddy (1978) observed that the teachers employed under private managements were the most satisfied while those in the government managements were the least satisfied. Similar results were obtained by Venkatarami Reddy and Baban (1980); and Venkatarami Reddy and Ramakrishnaiah (1981). In a comparative study of job satisfaction Tabatabai (1981) revealed that private sector employees were more satisfied with their job than public sector employees.

Results of Dodge's (1983) study revealed that proclamation factors accounted for 33 per cent of the variance in job satisfaction while the personal variables accounted for 2 per cent of the variance.

Saxana (1989) found that the teachers in schools with open climate are likely to show higher overall job satisfaction than their counterparts in closed climate schools.

Basha (1994) found that job satisfaction was significantly more among the public sector employees than those in private and co-operation management. Further, subjects from the private and co-operative sector did not differ in their job satisfaction.

Zaffane (1994) found that satisfaction increases when greater certainty about future directions or outcomes of the organizations is experienced and when job in certainty perceive positive work group performance.

Rana (1994) found that communication was one of the critical area in the whole process. It was most prominent by its absence, and consequently intended to be a major source of dissatisfaction.

Maheswar Panda (2002) conducted a study on job satisfaction of teachers in the context of types of management. He found that there is no significant difference between government teachers and private teachers in respect of their job satisfaction. And the college teachers, in general as well as both categories were satisfied with their job.

Sabarwal (2003) also observed that most of the dissatisfied teachers felt that there was a lack of communication between teachers and administrators.

Vijayalakshmi (2005) conducted a study and the findings showed, low and positive correlation between teacher effectiveness and job satisfaction. Only management of the school has significant impact both on teacher effectiveness and job satisfaction. The other variables included in the study viz., locality, subjects of teaching has no significant impact on both teacher effectiveness and job satisfaction.

Maheswar Thalkur (2007), concluded that correlates of job satisfaction for the high and low groups of the management level. The obtained highest percentage value for the high group is 86.19 and the lowest percentage value is 44.19. He found that 'management' is the most prominent correlates of job satisfaction for the high group of Secondary School Principals.

SELF-CONCEPT

Meaning

Self-concept is an idea of the self-constructed from believes one holds about oneself and the responses of others. Is the mental and conceptual understanding and persistent regard that sentient beings hold for their own existence. In other words, it is the sum total of a being's knowledge and understanding of his or her self the self-concept is different from self-consciousness, which is an awareness or pre-occupation with one's self. Components of self-concept include physical and psychological and social attributes, which can be influenced by the individuals attitudes, habits, beliefs and ideas. These components and attributes cannot be condensed to the general concepts of self-image and the self-esteem.

Definitions

An individuals perception of himself, as a person, which includes his abilities, appearance, performance in his job, and phases of daily living (Good, C.V., 1973).

Self-concept refers to the picture or image a person has of himself. (R.P. Taneja, 1991 and a group of experts, 2003)

Judge and Bono (2001) presented a meta-analysis showing that components of a positive self-concept construct were among the best predictors of job performance and job satisfaction.

The Impact of Self-Concept on the Job Satisfaction

Uma (1986) found that self-concept and sense of competence significantly moderated the work variables-job satisfaction relationship. It was also found that job involvement was significantly moderated by self concept.

Sharma (1999) investigated the relationship between type of personality based on Guna and self-concept and Job satisfaction. A sample of 74 males and females of varying ages and jobs and with at least 3 years of experience were administered; the self-concept inventory was developed by Basavanna in (1974) the scale of job satisfaction (Daftuar 1988) and a shorter version of the Personality Inventory (Pathak Bhatt and Sharma, 1992). Results revealed that sattva personality was positively correlated with self-concept but not satisfaction. Rajas personality was positively correlated with self-concept but negatively job satisfaction. Guna's self-concept and job satisfaction showed a positive significant relationship.

Cowin, L S, Johnson, M, Craven R G and Marsh, H W (2003) found that the self-concept of Nurses' was found to have a stronger association with nurses' retention plans ($B = .45$) than job satisfaction ($B = .28$). Aspects of pay and task were not significantly related to retention plans, however, professional status ($r = .51$), and to a lesser extent, organizational policies ($r = .27$) were significant factors.

Nurses' general self-concept was strongly related (r =.57) to retention plans.

PERSONALITY

The study of personality seeks to discover the reasons for a wide range of human behaviours, to account for their occurrence, and to assess their roles in the total person (Gordon, 1963). When the demographic and situational factors are capable of influencing the individual's satisfaction in either way, one's personality will certainly play a vital role in determining the job satisfaction/ dissatisfaction. As rightly pointed out by Vroom (1964) any study of job satisfaction should include both sets of variables viz., work role and personality variables.

Meaning and Definition

There are so many definitions of personality as it covers a varied and complex domain. In order to know the nature of personality some important definitions are discussed hereunder:

In general some define personality as "one's social stimulus value". Others define it as, "the sum total of innate dispositions, impulses, appetites, instincts, tendencies and habits". Another type of definition says that "personality is more than the sum of its parts and that more than is its pattern or organization". Some people define personality as "an individual's characteristic pattern of adjustment".

According to Cattel (1950), "Personality is that which permits a prediction of what person will do in a given situation".

Guilford (1954) says that an individual's personality is "an integrated pattern of traits". He defined personality, as "an individual's personality is unique pattern of traits. A trait is any distinguishable, relatively enduring way in which one individual differs from another".

Koul's (1974) definition on personality is that "it is an organization and integration of a large number of habits".

Crowne (1979) defined—personality is the organized system of potentialities for behaviour.

Madhuraj (1996), John Belling Ham, 2004 defined—personality is a psychological term that refers to the predictable and unique indicators of the way an individual might respond to the environment. A personal reference that usually connotes acceptability and likability.

The Impact of the Personality on the Job Satisfaction

The study of personality seeks to discover the reasons for a wide range of human behaviours, to account for their occurrence, and to access their roles in the total person (Gordon, 1963). When the demographic and situational factors are capable of influencing the individual's satisfaction in either way, one's personality will certainly play a vital role in determining the job satisfaction / dissatisfaction. As rightly pointed out by Vroom (1964) any study of job satisfaction should include both sets of variables viz., work role and personality variables.

Blum and Naylor (1968) observed that security must be considered as an important dimension of personality as it affects job satisfaction. An insecure person will remain insecure even though his job is secure. Family background and many similar factors contribute to the individual's security.

McCanaughy and Palmer (1969) found that personality traits of federal field executives in South California were significantly related to their job satisfaction.

Gupta (1977) made an attempt to see the personality structure of the primary school teachers. It was found that on factors E, F and Q_3 of 16 personality factors of Cattell, the subjects were slightly deviant and on factor 'N' they were strongly **deviant** and on the rest of the factors, they took average positions.

Heckert (1977) found that personal ideology influences behaviour and job satisfaction more than do the perceived press of peer group or organization. Hence, it was conjectured that external influences upon behaviour are mediated by the isolation of the classroom. Within the classroom teachers behave more consistently with personal beliefs than they do in areas of high visibility. Anand (1977) observed that it is the personality of a person which determines job satisfaction in the profession of school teaching.

Studies conducted by Hoppock (1935), Gellmon (1939), Kates (1950), Inlow (1951), and Blum (1956) showed that there was a positive relationship between personality factors and job satisfaction. On the other hand, according to Hulin (1977) the relationships among personality measures and job satisfaction had shown no trends which were of sufficient generality to be summarized. Similarly Hughes (1972) reported that employed subjects did not possess consistently the personality orientation appropriate to their jobs; and when the subjects were classified into groups as 'consistent' and 'inconsistent', it was found that there was no significant difference between the two mean job satisfaction scores.

Kuhn's (1982) study on teacher personality type and job satisfaction, indicated that extroverts tended to be more satisfied with their careers than introvert teachers. There tended to be higher mean satisfaction indicated by teachers having extrovert, sensing and judging characteristics.

Malik (1984) made a comparative study of personality factors and teaching environments of successful and unsuccessful teachers in selected schools of Rajasthan. The main objective of this study is to find out the inter-relationship between personality and factors of teachers and their attitude towards teaching profession. The findings reveal that personality, learning environment, concomitants, teaching success, attitude towards teaching, age and experience were some of the factor patterns associated with teaching.

Smart, Elton and Mc Langhim (1986) found that person environment congruence was positively related to the intrinsic job satisfaction of the men and women.

Balakrishna Reddy (1990) from his study on school teachers concluded that difference in the scores on personality factors do not affect the job satisfaction of the teachers, but the factors-I, M and Q_3 of the 16-personality factors influencing the job involvement of the subjects.

Ramakrishnaiah and Manjuvani (1999) from the study on college teachers job satisfaction identified a significant relationship between some of the personality characterstics viz, C, L and O of the 16-personality factors.

Carroll Bryan Shannon (2001) conducted a study on the effects of differential personality traits on student teacher performance and satisfaction. The results of this study indicated that based upon the criterion measures employed, differences in personality traits between student teachers and cooperating teachers were not effective predictors of student teacher performance or satisfaction. Upon further analyses of the data, it appeared that student teacher personality traits themselves were more predictive of their performance and satisfaction than were cooperating teacher personality traits or differences between personalities.

JOB INVOLVEMENT

Meaning of Job involvement

Job involvement may influence one's satisfaction with his job. The emphasis placed on job satisfaction variables has resulted in a relative neglect of the job involvement variable. This is perhaps due to a lack of conceptual differentiation between job satisfaction and job involvement and to an apparent failure to realize that it was possible for some persons to be highly satisfied, but not involved and for others to be highly involved, but not satisfied. Some sources of job satisfaction are probably more likely to be related to job involvement than others.

Definitions of Job involvement

Allport (1947) defined job involvement as "the situation in which the person engages the status seeking motive".

Lodehl (1964) explained job involvement as "the importance of work to a person's self-esteem or sense of worth". The job involved person is one for whom work is a very important part of life.

Causes of Job Involvement

Researchers who have defined job involvement as form of the performance—self-esteem contingency argue that intrinsic need satisfaction is a necessary condition for job involvement. Vroom (1962) proposed that a person's attempts to satisfy the need for self-esteem through work on the job leads to job involvement. In his study Vroom found that the degree of job involvement by his choice of ego rather than extrinsic factors help in describing the sources of satisfaction and dissatisfaction on the job.

Patchen (1970) identified three general conditions for job involvement. According to him, "Where people are highly motivated, where they feel a sense of solidarity with the enterprise, and where they get a sense of pride for their work, we may speak of them as highly involved in their job."

When Patchen talks of workers being highly motivated, he refers to their high levels of achievements need or to their wish to accomplish worthwhile things on the job. When he talks of workers solidarity with the enterprise, he refers to their need for belonging to the organization. Finally, when he talks of worker's sense of pride, he refers to workers 'feeling of high self-esteem'. Thus in Patchen's view, when a job provides opportunities for the satisfaction on one's achievement needs, belonging needs and self-esteem needs, one experiences a greater degree of job involvement.

Researchers who are in favour of defining job involvement as a central component of self-image consider job involvement to be caused by early socialization on the individual. However, they still maintain that intrinsic need satisfaction is an important precondition for job involvement.

Lawler and Hall (1970) are also in favour of defining job involvement as the psychological identification with the work. They believe that job involvement is partly caused by an individual's personal background and situations.

The above review of the causes of job involvement shows that almost all researchers consider intrinsic need satisfaction as the necessary condition for job involvement. The satisfaction of intrinsic needs of workers can be achieved only through appropriate changes in the job and the organizational environment.

Such changes like job variety, autonomy, opportunity for participation have also been viewed as situational factors causing job involvement. Besides the situational variables at the workplace that affect intrinsic motivation, researchers have also identified the protestant–work–ethic attitude as a cause of job involvement.

The protestant–work–ethic attitude is largely determined by post-socialisation processes experienced by individuals in specific socio-economic and cultural milieu in which they live. Thus, the rural / urban, blue collar / white collar and ethno-cultural backgrounds of individuals have been considered as cuases of job involvement. Thus, Roibinwitz and Hall (1977) consider the protestant–work–ethic attitude as a personal factor or individual-difference variable causing job involvement.

Studies on Job Involvement

Harding (1964) observed that those who had more opportunities of participation in the job are more receptive to organizational change.

Bass (1965) views it as representatives of the employee's ego involvement in his job and thus relates it to performance. Bass finds that the following conditions lead to the strengthening of job involvement: (1) opportunity to make more of the job decisions, (2) the feeling that one is making an important contribution to company's success, (3) recognition, (4) achievement, (5) self-determination and (6) freedom to set one's own workplace.

Lodahl and Kejner (1965) found that persons characterised by high job involvement tended to be organizational involved also. They also defined job involvement at two contexts in their article. In the first context they defined "it is the degree to which a person is identified psychologically with his work, or the importance of work in his total self-image". In the second context they defined, "it is the degree to which a person's work performance affects his self-esteem".

White (1966) found that those who had left the profession reported that they were significantly less job involved while employed, than those who remained within the profession.

According to Katz and Khan (1966), the implications of job involvement are as follows: (1) job involvement is a necessary condition if the individual is to accept fully the organizational demands placed upon him by his membership in an organization. (2) the degree of job involvement is related to the level of aspiration and the degree of internalization of organizational goals and (3) job involvement is a moderator variable in the relationship between satisfaction and performance.

Wissenberg and Gruenfeld (1968) considered job involvement to be a quasi-indicator of motivation. They also hypothesized that job satisfaction was one of the determinants of job involvement. The result showed that job involvement was related to satisfaction with recognition, achievement, responsibility and with interpersonal relations with the supervisor.

Lawler and Hall (1970) found that job satisfaction and job involvement were factorial independent and relatively district variables.

Marr and Marthur (1973) observed that Teacher Educators have key role in the involvement of education.

Gannon and Hendrickson (1973) found that "Career Orientation Job Involvement" was positively and significantly related to job satisfaction.

Wood (1974) supported the hypothesis that significant relationship occur more frequently between job satisfaction and job involvement.

Gechman and Wiener (1975) indicated that there was a positive association between job involvement and time devoted to work-related activities, but the time and job satisfaction were unrelated.

It was found by Cohen (1977) that the degree of participation in the job actions was largely motivated by job consciousness. Thus, it can be concluded that the association between the two variables is contradictory from situation to situation.

The relationship between job characteristics and job involvement was explored by Castro (1986), found that women working in jobs rated high on job characteristics showed limited job involvement than those women working in jobs rated low on those characteristics.

Blan (1986) found that job involvement and organizational commitment as interactive predictors of absenteeism and tardiness behaviours in nurses.

Wagner, Ferris, Fandt and Wayne (1987) found that organizational tenure did not explain a significant proportion of variance in job involvement after removal of exogenous effects.

Job involved individuals differ from their lesser involved colleagues in several significant ways. They are more likely to describe their jobs more stimulating or higher in range of job characteristics, including variety, autonomy, task identity and feedback (Elloy et al., 1991).

AN APPRAISAL

It may be seen from the brief review of literature presented in the foregoing pages that a number of studies have been carried out on the relation between job satisfaction and job involvement towards teaching and other variables. The studies yielded contradictory results on the relation between different personal and demographic variables and job satisfaction. Therefore it is difficult to summarise the conclusions of these studies as they have concerned themselves about a wide variety of aspects of job satisfaction, involvement and self-concept.

Although job satisfaction and job involvement are also important from the educational point of view, these areas are not much explored in relation with Teacher Educators. The results of even the few studies present a confusing picture with contradictory results.

It is needless to say that a very few studies have been conducted to study the job satisfaction of Teacher Educators. Whatever studies exists, none of them is comprehensive enough so as to enable one to draw any conclusive result.

Under these circumstances, it is quite reasonable to say that there is a great need to conduct more and more similar studies. Hence, thc investigator was made to move in this direction and conduct the investigation in which the job satisfaction of Teacher Educators working in various institutions. This resulted, finally into the statement of the present problem whose procedure of investigation is described in the following chapter.

CHAPTER 3

THE PRESENT STUDY

This chapter deals with statement of the problem, Title of the problem, Need for the study, Purpose of the study, Scope of the study, Definitions of the terms, Objectives, Hypotheses of the study and variables included in the study.

INTRODUCTION

From the time teaching started to gain recognition as a profession, experts as well as common men began to wonder about the effectiveness of the teacher.

P.N. DAVE

The expansion of pre-service Teacher Education to meet the needs of unprecedented expansion of education in the post independence period and the increased focus on inservice education of teachers on a continuous basis brought in its wake concomitant problems relating to the quality of Teacher Education in the country.

Research in Teacher Education is vast in its scope but it does not have a long past. The effective use of the dictionary is also a research topic the researcher is able to take up the study. Teacher Education departments and some of the national bodies in India are only focusing on this area but in countries like Australia has research unit in every department and there is a specified degree for each subject teaching. These facilities give the scope of understanding the field very clearly.

'Researchers working in Teacher Education area have brought into their study a wide spectrum of variables. If one has studied selection procedures, another has developed curriculum for Teacher Education programs and a third has tried to find out the effect of innovative instructional procedures on teacher effectiveness. This is largely due to the fact that Teacher Education is a long, complicated series of operations. Each operation, in itself, is an extremely complex set of steps. All these interact almost simultaneously'.

Fourth survey of education

The research on Teacher Educators is one of the most neglected areas in our country. One cannot found many studies on their quality, qualification and ability to do research in the field of education. Teacher Educators are working to develop quality by neglecting their own education. That may be the reason, even after 50 years, our system of education is not need based to meet the demands of the local community. Preparing a teacher to teach effectively is a technical job and Teacher Educator will get satisfaction by bringing the change in the student teachers in the classroom.

STATEMENT OF THE PROBLEM

The present study is to investigate the job satisfaction of Teacher Educators working in B.Ed colleges and also to know the relationship between the job satisfaction and job involvement. It is also aimed at to find the relation of job satisfaction of Teacher Educators with the various psycho-sociological variables.

TITLE OF THE PROBLEM

The title of the present study is, *"Job Satisfaction of B.Ed. Teacher Educators"*.

NEED FOR THE STUDY

Teacher Education today is an integral part of any educational system. Teaching, being both a skill and an art was found amenable to transmission in the early years of the 19th century. Mass literacy goals as well as the emergence of technology transformed the very character of teacher training and its philosophy. The National Policy on Education, 1986, reflects precisely this change in its concept and practice. No wonder then that Teacher Education has emerged as an important area of educational research.

As the review of related literature revealed that job satisfaction is an important area of study. The job of Teacher Educator is different from that of the school teacher. Therefore, the studies have to be done with respect to job analysis, role performance, job satisfaction, etc., of the Teacher Educator.

Number of Teacher Educators is increasing in this state and fresh postgraduates are entering into the system. Majority of the private institutions entered into Teacher Education field. There is a need to study the satisfactory level of the Teacher Educators in this new situation. In general the opinion is that the teachers are not satisfied with their job because it is low-paid job and their involvement is also too low in their job but in the level of higher education it is not a valid statement.

Higher education teacher is well paid but comparatively with software engineers in the present technology era it is low. Self-concept will play a major role in guiding the activities of the person. There is a need to study the relationship between self-concept and job satisfaction. The scholars in this area do not yet study it properly.

Human resource industry is not prospering in this country. There is a need to investigate the involvement of these Teacher Educators to develop the teaching skills among the prospective teachers. There is also a need to study the personality characters of the teacher educators in this state.

Teacher Educator is going to play a major role in shaping the mind of the society because teacher is the mind of the society. These Teacher Educators are minority group in the education system. They required strong commitment to influence the system of education. So there is a need to study the Teacher Educator to make him comfortable in the system to contribute some thing to the system.

PURPOSE OF THE STUDY

The present study aims at investigating the job satisfaction of Teacher Educators working in B.Ed colleges.

The purpose of the study is an attempt to answer the following aspects:

- Whether there is any relationship between job satisfaction of Teacher Educators with their job involvement?
- Whether there is any relationship between job satisfaction and self-concepts of the Teacher Educators?
- Whether there is any relation between job satisfaction and socio-demographic variables of Teacher Educators?
- Whether there is any relationship between job satisfaction and self-concepts of the Teacher Educators?
- Whether there is any relationship between job satisfaction and personality characteristics of the Teacher Educators?

It is possible to predict the job satisfaction of Teacher Educators with the help of different sets of variables namely socio-demographic, self-concepts, job involvement and personality factors.

SCOPE OF THE STUDY

The main intention of the study is to know the level of job satisfaction of Teacher Educators working in B.Ed colleges in the state of Andhra Pradesh.

The present study is also interested to know the relationship between job satisfaction and job involvement. Various socio-demographic variables are considered and their influence on job satisfaction is studied. The influence of region and management of the college on job satisfaction is also investigated. The influence of the psychological variables namely self-concepts and personality factors on job satisfaction is studied. With the help of different sets of variables; the job satisfaction of Teacher Educators is predicted.

DEFINITIONS OF THE TERMS

The Definitions of some of the important terms used in this investigation are given below.

(i) Job

Campbell, Lawler (1970) defined "A job is not an entity or a physical thing but a complex of inter-relationships of likes, roles, responsibilities, interactions, incentives and rewards".

The term used vocational guidance meaning the process of determining the features and details of particular job or the nature of the tasks required within a certain occupational area (John Bellingham, 2004).

(ii) Job Satisfaction

Campbell Lawler (1970) defined the term as "job satisfaction has been used in a variety of ways. Job satisfaction is a pleasurable or positive emotional state resulting from the appraisal of one's job experiences."

Bhuyan (2005) defined the term as "job satisfaction is a set of favorable or unfavorable feelings and emotion with which employees view their work. Job satisfaction typically refers to attitudes of a particular employee but assessments of individual employees' satisfaction can be averaged by looking at overall performance of all the members of an organization."

The extent, to which a job provides general satisfaction to the worker, meets personal and/or professional needs and goals and is congruent with personal values. From the point of view of salary; from the point of view of status; from the point of general surroundings; from the point of view of social position or from all these combined. Actually job satisfaction can come only after one has entered in the job (John Bellingham, 2004).

(iii) Job Involvement

Blan (1986) found that job involvement and organizational commitment as interactive predictors of absenteeism and tardiness behaviors in nurses.

Wagner, Ferris, Fandt and Wayne (1987) found that organizational tenure did not explain a significant proportion of variance in job involvement after removal of exogenous effects.

Job involved individuals differ from their lesser-involved colleagues in several significant ways. They are more likely to describe their jobs more stimulating or higher in range of job characteristics, including variety, autonomy, task identity and feedback (Dlloy et al., 1991).

(iv) Teacher

A person employed in an official capacity for the purpose of guiding and directing the learning experiences of pupils or students in an educational institution, whether public or private (Good, 1973).

A person engaged by an educational institution to instruct others. In public or government school, a person who has completed a minimum programme of professional teacher education and met other requirements to qualify for state certificate as a teacher any one carrying on instruction. A person who instructs students. (John Bellingham, 2004).

(v) Self-concept

An individual's perception of himself, as a person, which includes his abilities, appearance, performance in his job, and phases of daily living (Good, C.V., 1973).

How a person sees himself (e.g. competent, amusing, homely, etc.). This may differ from other people's views of him though they will have influenced it (Derek Rowntree, 1981).

(i) An individual perception of self (ii) A psychological contract that is more complexes than implied or assumed by most educators. (Madhu Raj, 1996).

Self-concept refers to the picture or image a person has of himself. (R.P. Taneja, 1991 and A group of experts, 2003).

(vi) Personality

A psychological term that refers to the predictable and unique indicators of the way an individual might respond to the environment. A personal reference that usually connotes acceptability and likability (Madhu Raj, 1996, John Bellingham, 2004).

Personality traits are defined as "generalized and personalized determining tendencies—consistent and stable modes of an individuals adjustment to their environment" (John, 1999; Allport and Odbert).

OBJECTIVES OF THE STUDY

The study has been designed with the following specific objectives:

1. To identify the level of job satisfaction of Teacher Educators working in B.Ed. colleges.
2. To know the level of relationship of job satisfaction and job involvement of Teacher Educators.
3. To find the influence of sex and region on job satisfaction of Teacher Educators.
4. To know the interaction effect of sex and region on the job satisfaction of the Teacher Educators.
5. To find out the effect of socio-demographic variables on job satisfaction.

6. To find out the influence of self-concepts on job satisfaction.
7. To identify the influence of personality factors on job satisfaction.
8. To predict the job satisfaction with the help of different sets of variables namely socio-demographic variables, self-concepts and personality factors.
9. To predict the job satisfaction with the help of all the variables in the investigation.
10. To develop multiple regression equations in order to predict the job satisfaction of Teacher Educators.

HYPOTHESES TO BE TESTED

In the light of the above objectives, the following major Null hypotheses have been set up for the purpose of this investigation.

1. The Teacher Educators working in B.Ed. colleges would not satisfy with their jobs.
2. There would be no significant relation between job satisfaction and job involvement of the Teacher Educators.
3. There would be no significant influence of the main effects Sex and Region on job satisfaction of Teacher Educators.
4. There is no significant interaction effect of sex and region on the job satisfaction.
5. Socio-demographic variables do not influence the job satisfaction of Teacher Educators.
6. Self-concept would not have significant influence on job satisfaction.
7. Personality of the Teacher Educators would not have significant bearing on job satisfaction.
8. It would not be possible to predict the job satisfaction of Teacher Educators with the help of the different

sets of variables namely socio-demographic variables, self-concepts and personality factors.

9. It could not be possible to predict job satisfaction with the help of all the variables in the investigation.
10. It could not be possible to develop the regression equations to predict job satisfaction with the help of independent variables of the present investigation.

VARIABLES INCLUDED IN THE STUDY

The problem envisages an investigation of, *"Job Satisfaction of B.Ed Teacher Educators"*. The job satisfaction is studied in relation to certain psycho-socio-demographic variables. The psycho-socio-demographic variables are given here below.

Dependent Variable

Job satisfaction of Teacher Educators is taken as dependent variable. The scores on the job satisfaction scale developed by the investigator will serve for the purpose of measuring the dependent variable.

Independent Variables

The independent variables are studied under four sub-headings:

(*i*) **Socio-demographic variables:** The following socio-demographic variables have studied in this investigation.

1. Sex
2. Age
3. Qualification
4. Teaching experience
5. Marital Status
6. Occupation of spouse
7. Total salary per month

8. Annual Income
9. Region
10. Management
11. Total members in the family
12. Religion
13. Caste.

(*ii*) **Self-concepts:** The scale developed by Dr. (Miss) Mukta Rastogi (1974) was adopted. There are 10 areas in the scale. They are:

14. Self concept A : Health and sex appropriateness
15. Self Concept B : Abilities
16. Self Concept E : Self confidence
17. Self Concept F : Self acceptance
18. Self Concept H : Worthyness
19. Self Concept P : Present, past and future
20. Self Concept S_1 : Beliefs and convictions
21. Self Concept S_2 : Feelings of shame and guilt
22. Self Concept S_3 : Sociability
23. Self Concept S_4 : Emotional

(*iii*) **Personality factors:** Cattell's 16 personality factors questionnaire (1970) was adopted. The personality factors are:

Descriptors of Low Range	Primary Factor	Descriptors of High Range
Impersonal, distant, cool, reserved, detached, formal, aloof (Schizothymia)	Warmth (A)	Warm, outgoing, attentive to others, kindly, easy going, participating, likes people (Affectothymia)

Descriptors of Low Range	Primary Factor	Descriptors of High Range
Concrete thinking, lower general mental capacity, less intelligent, unable to handle abstract problems (Lower Scholastic Mental Capacity)	Reasoning (B)	Abstract-thinking, more intelligent, bright, higher general mental capacity, fast learner (Higher Scholastic Mental Capacity)
Reactive emotionally, changeable, affected by feelings, emotionally less stable, easily upset (Lower Ego Strength)	Emotional Stability (C)	Emotionally stable, adaptive, mature, faces reality calmly (Higher Ego Strength)
Deferential, cooperative, avoids conflict, submissive, humble, obedient, easily led, docile, accommodating (Submissiveness)	Dominance (E)	Dominant, forceful, assertive, aggressive, competitive, stubborn, bossy (Dominance)
Serious, restrained, prudent, taciturn, introspective, silent (Desurgency)	Liveliness (F)	Lively, animated, spontaneous, enthusiastic, happy, go lucky, cheerful, expressive, impulsive (Surgency)
Expedient, nonconforming, disregards rules, self indulgent (Low Super Ego Strength)	Rule-Consciousness (G)	Rule-conscious, dutiful, conscientious, conforming, moralistic, staid, rule bound (High Super Ego Strength)
Shy, threat-sensitive, timid, hesitant, intimidated (Threctia)	Social Boldness (H)	Socially bold, venturesome, thick skinned, uninhibited (Parmia)
Utilitarian, objective, unsentimental, tough minded, self-reliant, no-nonsense, rough (Harria)	Sensitivity (I)	Sensitive, aesthetic, sentimental, tender minded, intuitive, refined (Premsia)

Descriptors of Low Range	Primary Factor	Descriptors of High Range
Trusting, unsuspecting, accepting, unconditional, easy (Alaxia)	Vigilance (L)	Vigilant, suspicious, skeptical, distrustful, oppositional (Protension)
Grounded, practical, prosaic, solution oriented, steady, conventional (Praxernia)	Abstractedness (M)	Abstract, imaginative, absent minded, impractical, absorbed in ideas (Autia)
Forthright, genuine, artless, open, guileless, naive, unpretentious, involved (Artlessness)	Privateness (N)	Private, discreet, nondisclosing, shrewd, polished, worldly, astute, diplomatic (Shrewdness)
Self-Assured, unworried, complacent, secure, free of guilt, confident, self satisfied (Untroubled)	Apprehension (O)	Apprehensive, self doubting, worried, guilt prone, insecure, worrying, self blaming (Guilt Proneness)
Traditional, attached to familiar, conservative, respecting traditional ideas(Conservatism)	Openness to Change (Q1)	Open to change, experimental, liberal, analytical, critical, free thinking, flexibility (Radicalism)
Group-oriented, affiliative, a joiner and follower dependent (Group Adherence)	Self-Reliance (Q2)	Self-reliant, solitary, resourceful, individualistic, self sufficient (Self-Sufficiency)
Tolerates disorder, unexacting, flexible, undisciplined, lax, self-conflict, impulsive, careless of social rules, uncontrolled (Low Integration)	Perfectionism (Q3)	Perfectionistic, organized, compulsive, self-disciplined, socially precise, exacting will power, control, self-sentimental (High Self-Concept Control)
Relaxed, placid, tranquil, torpid, patient, composed low drive (Low Ergic Tension)	Tension (Q4)	Tense, high energy, impatient, driven, frustrated, over wrought, time driven. (High Ergic Tension)

(iv) Job Involvement Score

Total number of independent variables in present investigation is fortyone (13+11+16+1=41).

LIMITATIONS OF THE STUDY

The following limitations are observed in this investigation.

1. The present study is limited to the Teacher Educators working in B.Ed colleges.
2. This study is confirmed to the state of Andhra Pradesh only.
3. Job satisfaction is related to number of psycho–socio–demographic and other variables. Limited numbers of variables are studied in this investigation.
4. This is only a presage-product investigation in the area of job satisfaction.
5. Due to difficulties in data collection, only limited number of sample subjects is included in this investigation.
6. Due to laborious calculations only certain variables are studied in this investigation.
7. It is a survey type of research, where in the techniques of questionnaires are employed.

CHAPTER 4

METHODS OF INVESTIGATION

This chapter describes the methods employed in the measurement of the variables, selection of the sample, collection of data, scoring the responses, analysis of the data and statistical techniques employed.

The flow chart showing the procedure followed in the present investigation is shown in Figure 4.1.

MEASUREMENT OF VARIABLES

Out of the 42 variables (both dependent and independent) investigated in the present study, 13 are personal and demographic variables for which information was gathered through a personal data sheet and the remaining 29 variables were measured with suitable instruments. A brief description of the instruments employed is given in the following pages.

INSTRUMENTS USED IN THE PRESENT STUDY

The following instruments are used in the present study

1. Job Satisfaction Inventory (JSI)
2. Job Involvement Inventory (JII)
3. Self-Concept Scale (SCS)
4. Cattell's Personality Questionnaire (From 'C') (CPQ)
5. Socio-Demographic Scale (SDS)

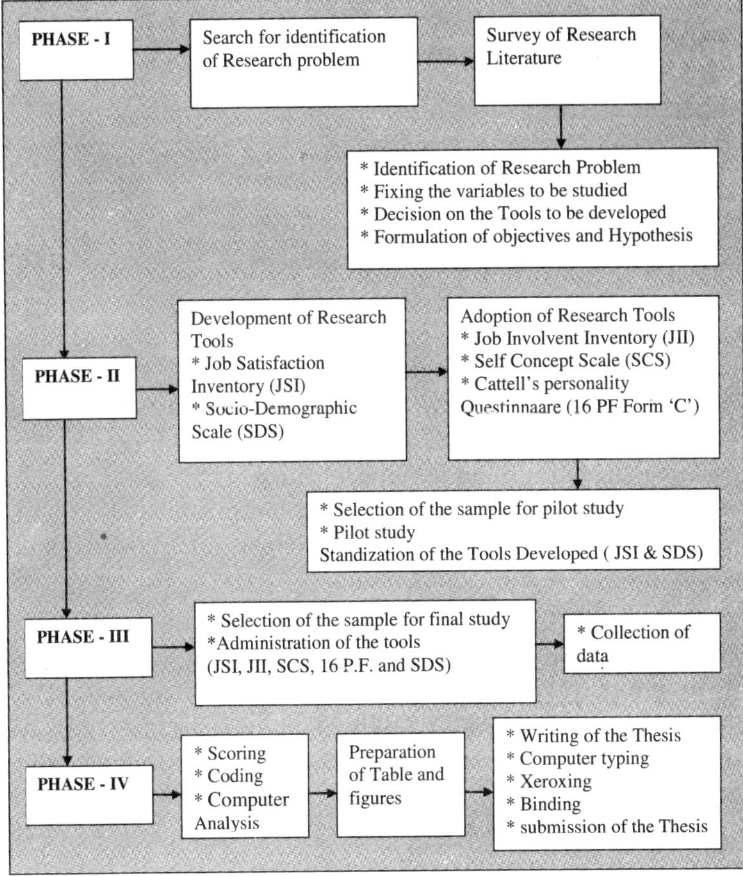

Fig. 4.1. Flow Chart showing the procedures followed in the present investigation

Job Satisfaction Inventory

The Job Satisfaction Inventory is discussed under the following headings

1. Different methods of measuring job satisfaction
2. Meaning of Job Satisfaction
3. Construction of the preliminary form
4. Pilot Study: item analysis

5. Factor analysis
6. Selection of items for final form

Different Methods of Measuring Job Satisfaction

Among the various procedures used to measure job satisfaction, the most often used are: interviews, projective techniques, and attitude questionnaires (Hoppock, 1960; Kirkpatrick, 1962); Ketzell, 1964; Johnson, 1967; Blum and Naylor, 1948; and 1968). Among the three again, the best questionnaires constructed on the basis of attitude scalling methodology with evaluative type of items (Ketzell, 1964; Blum and Naylor, 1968). That is, Job satisfaction is operationally measured by obtaining the subjects verbal rating of his job or of its various features on a scale of hedonic tone ('like–dislike' or 'satisfactory–unsatisfactory', etc.). This means that the existence of one or more distinct dimensions of evaluation may be shown to be reflected in the items and a scoring method must be devised which weights each response in terms of the degree of affect expressed on a given dimension (Blum and Naylor, 1968). Job satisfaction questionnaires meeting these specifications can be instructed on any of the standard attitude scale rationales, such of Likert (1932), Thurstone (1946) or Gutman (1947).

Meaning of Job Satisfaction

Job satisfaction is the result of various attitudes possessed by an employee (Blum and Naylor, 1968). In a narrow sense, their attitudes are related to the job and are concerned with such specific factors as: (1) Wages, (2) Supervision, (3) Steadiness of employment, (4) Conditions of work, (5) Opportunities for advancement, (6) Recognition of ability, (7) Fair evaluation of work, (8) Social relations on the job, (9) Prompt settlement of grievances, (10) Fair treatment by employer, and (11) Other similar factors. Other aspects such as employee's age, health, temperament and level of aspirations should also be considered. Against his family relationships, social status activities in other organizations—labour, political or social contribute ultimately, to his job satisfaction.

In his study on job satisfaction, Hoppock (1953) proposed the following six major components of job satisfaction:

(*a*) The way the individual reacts to unpleasant situations,

(*b*) The facility with which he adjusts himself to other persons,

(*c*) His relative status in the social and economic group with which he identifies himself,

(*d*) The nature of the work in relation to his abilities, interests and preparation for the Job,

(*e*) Security

(*f*) Loyalty.

According to Blum and Naylor (1968), these six items are not of the minute or specific characters measured in many studies on job satisfaction; possibly that is what is wrong with these studies. Hoppock's approach is to be commended for this reason that he is aware of the real factors which contribute to job satisfaction and does not get lost in the petty details.

Vroom (1964) listed the following seven dimensions which go into job satisfaction:

(*a*) Attitude towards the company and company management,

(*b*) Attitude towards promotional opportunities,

(*c*) Attitude towards job content,

(*d*) Attitude towards supervision,

(*e*) Attitude towards financial rewards,

(*f*) Attitude towards working conditions,

(*g*) Attitude towards co-workers.

According to Katzel (1964) job satisfaction is the expression of an incumbent's evaluation of his job. In short, job satisfaction is an attitude which is the result of many specific attitudes in three areas, viz., specific job factors, individual characteristics and group relationship outside the job.

Construction of the Preliminary Form

Bearing the above important dimensions of job satisfaction in mind, a number of items (opinions) that are related to job satisfaction of Teacher Educators were collected from a number of sources. Twenty-five men and Twenty-five women teacher educators were requested to write the factors in the form of statements which cause satisfaction or dissatisfaction to the Teacher Educators. These statements were sorted out and listed. This list of statements was supplemented by a careful study of related literature and informal interviews with teacher educators, and a pool of 150 items was prepared. The pool of items or universe of items as gutam (1947) calls it, thus collected was refined by observing the following criteria laid down by different authors i.e. Likert (1932), Edwards and Kilpatrick (1949), Guilford (1954) and others:

(*a*) The statements must be clear, precise and straightforward.

(*b*) They should be short and to the point.

(*c*) 'Double barreled' statements should be removed.

(*d*) They must be constructed as expressions of desired behavior, not as statement of fact.

(*e*) They must be in such a form that the ideas can be accepted or rejected.

(*f*) Both favorable and unfavorable statements must be included.

(*g*) Statements that could be endorsed by everyone or no one must be avoided.

(*h*) Negative and positive statements must be arranged randomly throughout the attitude scale so that any space error may be avoided.

The item pool thus refined was presented to 10 experienced men and women teacher educators who requested to:

(*a*) Add other statements that might be relevant to the subject

(*b*) Point out redundant statements,

(*c*) Mark ambiguous and 'double barreled' items, if any

(*d*) Give suggestions for refining the items.

Their suggestions were incorporated and 106 items were selected to be included in the preliminary form. The items were randomized. Each of the items was arranged on a five-point scale with the following alternatives—*Strongly Agree, Agree, Doubtful, Disagree and Strongly Disagree.* To avoid faking of the responses, the attitude scale was made anonymous. The items were translated into Telugu language and used for the pilot study.

Pilot Study

The pilot study was conducted on 222 Teacher Educators, selected by a multistage stratified random sampling procedure from 45 colleges of education belonging to Andhra Pradesh state. The sample was distributed among the three kinds of managements (government, private and minority) and three regions of the state. The pilot form of the job satisfaction inventory which is self-administering was administered to the sample of teacher educators individually in their respective colleges during leisure hours.

Even though the scale is self-administering as a matter of motivating the teacher educators, they were explained the purpose of the research, and the way they had to answer the items. They were also assured that the data would be used only for research work and would be kept confidential.

For the purpose of scoring, numerical weights were assigned as shown in Table 4.1, to each of the 5 categories of responses, viz., *Strongly Agree, Agree, Doubtful, Disagree and Strongly Disagree* as suggested by Likert (1932).

Table 4.1

Numerical Weights Given to the Five Alternative Responses

Type of statement	Strongly Agree	Agree	Doubtful	Disagree	Strongly Disagree
Positive	5	4	3	2	1
Negative	1	2	3	4	5

This method of assigning numerical weights to the responses is simple and highly satisfactory. Likert (1932) found that scores based upon this relatively simple assignment of integral weights correlated 0.99 with the complicated and time consuming normal deviate system of weighting.

After scoring the responses of the teacher educators as described above, item analysis was carried out by the method of criterion of internal consistency suggested by Likert (1932). The results obtained by this method of criterion of internal consistency agree very well with the results of the traditional method of item analysis, at the same time this method is far less laborious than the latter, and is advocated by many investigators like Likert (1932), Murphy and Likert (1937), Edwards (1969), to mention a few.

Selection of the Items

This method consists of rank ordering the respondents with respect to their total scores and taking a high group and a low group on the basis of the total score and calculating the internal consistency of each statement using the formula:

Internal consistency = The difference between the means of any statement scores of the high and low groups on the statement.

In the present analysis the highest scoring 27 per cent and lowest scoring 27 per cent were taken to present the criterion groups because with this tail proportions, the coefficient is most sensitive (Kelly, 1939). The Difference between the mean scores of high and low groups on each of the items was tested for significance by applying 't' test and 80 items for which the 't' value was significant at or above 0.05 level were selected to be included in the job satisfaction inventory.

Selection of Items for Final Study

The items with 't' values less than 1.98 were deleted. In this investigation 26 items were deleted and 80 items were retained for Final Study.

Out of 80 items in the final study, there are 33 positive items. The item numbers 4, 9, 25, 28, 29, 32, 33, 35, 36, 37, 39, 42, 45, 46, 49, 51, 52, 56, 62, 63, 64, 65, 67, 70, 74, 76, 77, 83, 84, 91, 94, 95 and 105 are positive. The remaining items (47 items) are negative.

For the calculation of the 't' values the procedure suggested by Edwards (1957) was followed.

The calculation 't' value for the item No. 76 of the pilot study inventory is shown in Table 4.2.

The 't' value of the items of the pilot study are presented in Table 4.3.

The main aim of the pilot study was to establish the validity and reliability of the Job Satisfaction inventory.

Table 4.2

The calculation of 't' value for evaluating the difference in the mean response to the item No. 76 of the pilot study of job satisfaction inventory for the high group and low group.

Response Categories	High Group				Low Group			
	x	f	fx	fx^2	x	f	fx	fx^2
Strongly Agree	5	31	155	775	5	16	80	400
Agree	4	27	108	432	4	16	64	256
Doubtful	3	-	0	0	3	6	18	54
Disagree	2	2	4	8	2	16	32	64
Strongly Disagree	1	-	0	0	1	6	6	6
Sums		60	267	1215		60	200	780

$$\bar{X}_H = \frac{\Sigma f(x)}{\Sigma f} = \frac{267}{60} = 4.45 \qquad \bar{X}_L = \frac{\Sigma f(x)}{\Sigma f} = \frac{200}{60} = 3.33$$

$$\Sigma(X_H - \bar{X_H})_2 = \Sigma f(x)^2 - \frac{(\Sigma f(x))^2}{\Sigma f} \qquad \Sigma(X_L - \bar{X_L})_2 = \Sigma f(x)^2 - \frac{(\Sigma f(x))^2}{\Sigma f}$$

$$= 1215 - \frac{(267)^2}{60} \qquad = 780 - \frac{(200)^2}{60}$$

$$= 1215 - 1188.15 \qquad = 780 - 666.66$$

$$= 26.85 \qquad = 113.34$$

$$t = \frac{(\bar{X}_H - \bar{X}_L)}{\sqrt{\frac{\Sigma) X_H - \bar{X}_H)^2 + \Sigma(X_L - \bar{X}_L)^2}{x}}}$$

$$= \frac{4.45 - 3.33}{\sqrt{\frac{26.85 + 113.34}{60 \times 59}}} = \frac{1.12}{\sqrt{\frac{140.19}{3540}}} = \frac{1.12}{0.19} = 5.89$$

$$t = 5.89$$

Table 4.3

The 't' value for all the items of the pilot study of Job Satisfaction Inventory

Item No.	't' Value	Remarks
1	1.47	Deleted
2	2.54	Retained
3	1.79	Deleted
4	3.11	Retained
5	0.38	Deleted
6	1.13	Deleted
7	0.97	Deleted
8	1.63	Deleted
9	2.81	Retained
10	0.16	Deleted
11	4.52	Retained
12	0.12	Deleted
13	1.45	Deleted
14	2.95	Retained
15	0.63	Deleted
16	3.96	Retained
17	0.55	Deleted
18	2.55	Retained
19	4.46	Retained
20	3.31	Retained
21	5.31	Retained
22	4.88	Retained
23	1.69	Deleted

Item No.	't' Value	Remarks
24	3.59	Retained
25	3.63	Retained
26	2.54	Retained
27	6.93	Retained
28	3.27	Retained
29	3.93	Retained
30	0.49	Deleted
31	3.34	Retained
32	2.39	Retained
33	2.41	Retained
34	2.45	Retained
35	2.26	Retained
36	2.19	Retained
37	2.27	Retained
38	3.22	Retained
39	3.57	Retained
40	0.14	Deleted
41	0.34	Deleted
42	4.39	Retained
43	5.50	Retained
44	2.46	Retained
45	2.75	Retained
46	4.14	Retained
47	8.49	Retained
48	2.65	Retained
49	4.80	Retained
50	3.60	Retained

Item No.	't' Value	Remarks
51	3.17	Retained
52	6.31	Retained
53	7.12	Retained
54	2.96	Retained
55	7.82	Retained
56	2.70	Retained
57	0.25	Deleted
58	1.86	Deleted
59	0.54	Deleted
60	1.79	Deleted
61	5.44	Retained
62	5.97	Retained
63	4.56	Retained
64	6.15	Retained
65	2.43	Retained
66	5.56	Retained
67	5.28	Retained
68	5.10	Retained
69	8.15	Retained
70	4.35	Retained
71	6.42	Retained
72	6.31	Retained
73	4.72	Retained
74	2.80	Retained
75	3.37	Retained
76	5.61	Retained
77	8.49	Retained
78	3.13	Retained

Item No.	't' Value	Remarks
79	5.03	Retained
80	3.73	Retained
81	5.57	Retained
82	6.24	Retained
83	3.83	Retained
84	3.20	Retained
85	4.21	Retained
86	0.06	Deleted
87	1.62	Deleted
88	3.30	Retained
89	6.31	Retained
90	1.77	Deleted
91	2.95	Retained
92	6.67	Retained
93	4.80	Retained
94	3.41	Retained
95	3.82	Retained
96	1.85	Deleted
97	1.95	Deleted
98	2.46	Retained
99	0.00	Deleted
100	5.79	Retained
101	4.09	Retained
102	5.10	Retained
103	2.18	Retained
104	5.75	Retained
105	4.26	Retained
106	1.65	Deleted

Validity

The validity of a test is concerned with the question of what is measured. "When used without qualification and when used in the practical setting, the term validity refers to the degree to which the test scores or other measure predict some practical criterion measures. In a broad sense validity has to do with the question what test scores measure and what they will predict?" (Guilford, 1954). There are various methods of estimating validity of a measuring instrument. For the purpose of this investigation, the following type of validity was established for the job satisfaction inventory.

Content Validity

"This form of validity is estimated by evaluating the relevance of the test items, individually and as a whole. Each item should be a sampling of the knowledge or performance, which the test purports to measure. Taken collectively, the items should constitute a representative sample of the variable to be tested. At the same time, it is essential that the content not be compounded by introducing irrelevant problems and materials" (Freeman, 1965). Validity of content should not depend upon the subjective judgment of only one specialist. In the construction of the inventory, therefore, the selection of items was based upon careful analysis, by several specialists, of related literature and empirical findings and actual subject matter. Care was taken in determining most significant topics and facts and areas. Representative items were also devised on the lines of the experts who constructed similar test items. The technical procedures followed by them were also studied. The review of related literature, interview with teachers, the analysis of items by experts and the best discrimination of items between individuals at the upper and lower levels contributed to the establishment of content validity. Thus content validation rested first upon the expert analysis of the materials to be sampled and second upon the use of available statistical procedures to refine original selection of items. Thus, it can be reasonably assumed that the inventory has content validity.

Item Validity

There are numerous indices and procedures for determining item validity. One of which stresses the number of discriminations of the desired sort that the item is capable of making. It emphasizing the content to which the item predicts segregation of examinees into those with high versus those with low criterion scores. The discriminative power of each of the items was established before including them in the final form. The 't' value calculated for each of the items is a measure of the extent to which a given statement differentiates between the high and low groups. Thus the items in the inventory with 't' values equal to or greater than 1.98 (at 0.05 level of significance for 118 df) ensure item validity of the inventory.

Intrinsic Validity

Guilford (1954) defined intrinsic validity as "the degree to which a test measures what it measures". This can also be stated in terms of how well the obtained scores measure the test's true score component. This validity is given by the square root of its reliability. Hence, the intrinsic validity of the job satisfaction inventory was $\sqrt{0.921} = 0.959$.

Criterion Validity

The total samples of teachers were classified into three groups on the basis of their answers to an overall item, given at the end of the scale. The three groups were, those who satisfied with their job, (1) less than others, (2) as much as others, and (3) more than others. The mean job satisfactions of the two extreme groups on the entire scale of 80 items were tested whether the difference between them was significant. It was found that the 't' was significant at 0.001 level. Therefore it could be concluded that the test is measuring what it purports to measure.

Face Validity

If the common thread of an attitude runs through all the scale items, the resultant scale has "Face validity" for that attitude. All the items in the attitude scale towards job satisfaction of Teacher Educators have common thread of attitude about the job satisfaction, so there is face validity in the job satisfaction inventory.

Concurrent Validity and Predictive Validity

In a situation of some observable criterion, the scale's validity can be investigated by seeing how good an indicator it is. This approach leads to two categories of validity, i.e., 'predictive validity' and 'concurrent validity'.

Predictive validity is concerned with how the scale can forecast a future criterion and concurrent validity with how well it can describe a present one. The results in the succeeding chapter show that the job satisfaction inventory has both concurrent validity and predictive validity.

Reliability

"Traditionally, the textbooks have told us that there are three fundamental types of approach to the estimation of reliability. All of these were designed to answer the question, 'what is the self-correction of this test? There have been three standard procedures, known loosely as the 'split-half', 'alternative forms', and 'retest' methods" (Guilford, 1954).

Selection of one of these reliability estimates depends upon the type of test and the meaning of the statistics or the purpose for which it is used. Generally, homogeneous tests shall have high degree of index of internal consistency. But whereas in a heterogeneous test, a high index of internal consistency would not be expected. The division of a test into two parts for this purpose is to be accomplished in a way that will ensure that the two resemble each other in a certain statistical way as well as in more superficial and obvious ways. Each should represent faithfully the total test in all significant respects. Then, another method for estimation of an approximate index of reliability for a heterogeneous test would be retest variety. This retest coefficient of correlation tells us nothing concerning the internal consistency of a test. The key concept for this procedure is that a stability. It answers the questions concerning how stable or dependable are the measurements over a period of time. High reliability of this kind tells us that the individuals remain rather uniform or maintain their rank of positions in spite of changes, in whatever psychological functions this test measure. "A low retest reliability coefficient means that the function or functions measured fluctuate from time to time or the test as an instrument is affected by other things that do fluctuate" (Guilford, 1954). These changes have been called 'function fluctuations' of individuals.

"The alternative methods bear resemblance to both the internal consistency and retest approach. The end results in an index of internal consistency... In the extreme time interval case, this is like resting; expect that it is with a different form of the same test. At any rate, the alternate forms method indicates both equivalence of content and suitability of performance" (Guilford, 1954).

However, the following two methods were applied in determining the reliability of the job satisfaction inventory.

(*i*) Split-half reliability and

(*ii*) Test-retest reliability

Split-half Reliability

"By means of this technique, which is used to find internal consistency, the items in a whole test are divided into two halves which should be equivalent or very nearly so. Thus the two scores, one for each half, are obtained for each individual by administering the test only once and each score is treated as though it represented a separate form" (Freeman, 1965). So the odd and even items were systematically arranged considering number sequences, vocabularies etc. The inventory with 80 items was split into two halves. The scores on the odd and even items were correlated on a sample of 222 Teacher Educators using Person's formula for product moment correlation. This gave the reliability of half test. The reliability of the half-test was 0.819. This was correlated for full length of the test by Spearman-Brown Prophecy Formula. The reliability of the full test thus obtained was 0.903.

The obtained internal consistency of the test is sufficient to consider the fitness of the test for any use. Kelley (1939) maintains that, "when a test is to be used for a group measurement purposes, a reliability coefficient of 0.50 of highest is needed".

Test-retest Reliability

In order to determine the test-retest reliability, the test was again administered on the sample of 111 Teacher Educators with a gap of 15 days. The test-retest reliability was found out by product moment correlation coefficient between the test and the retest scores. The obtained correlation coefficient between the test-retest scores was 0.928 which is significant at 0.01 level of confidence.

The reliability coefficients, 0.903 and 0.928 obtained by applying split-half method and test-retest method show high reliability of the job satisfaction inventory.

Job Involvement Inventory

Job involvement is the degree to which person identifies himself psychologically with his work. It is reflective of the importance of his work in his total self-image. Job involvement is the internalization of values about the goodness of the work. It measures the easy with which the person can be further socialized by the organization.

The process of ego involvement in work has been a great cancers for any researcher in the area of work performance and worker satisfaction (Mc. Gregor, 1944; Allport, 1947; Durbin, 1961) organizational conditions like meaningfulness of work, adequacy of supervision and other social aspects of work are important for the job involvement of any worker.

Job involvement acts as a moderator variable in interpreting the relationship between the job satisfaction and job performance. The degree of job involvement is influenced by the level of aspiration and the degree of internalization of organizational goals.

Job Satisfaction and Job Performance will be related in the case of persons who exhibit certain amount of job involvement. Decision to participate and decision to produce are also influenced by Job involvement according to March and Siman (1958).

Definitions of Job Involvement

Lodhal (1964) defined Job involvement as the importance of work to a person's self-esteem or sense of worth. He hypothesized that the main determinant of job involvement is a value orientation toward work that is learned early in the socialization process.

According to Kafz and Khan (1966) Job involvement is a necessary condition if one is to accept the organizational demands placed upon him.

Lawler and Hall (1970) opined that the Job involvement refers to the 'Psychological identification with one's work as well as the degree to which the job satisfaction is central to the person and his identity.

These Job involvements can be considered as an important measure or organizational effectiveness that may be, at least in part, influenced by Job Satisfaction.

Job Involvement

Job involvement may influence one's satisfaction with his job. The emphasis placed on job satisfaction variables has resulted in a relative neglect of the job involvement variables. This is perhaps due to a lack of conceptual differentiation between job satisfaction and job involvement and to an apparent failure to realize that it was possible for some persons to be highly satisfied, but not involved and for others to be highly involved, but not satisfied. Some sources of Job satisfaction are probably more likely to relate to job involvement than others.

Allport (1947) defined involvement as "the situation in which the person engages the status seeking motive".

Blan (1986) found that job involvement and organizational commitment as interactive predictors of absenteeism and tardiness behaviors in nurses.

Wagner, Ferris, Fandt and Wayne (1987) found that organizational tenure did not explain a significant proportion of variance in job involvement after removal of exogenous effects.

Job involved individuals differ from their lesser involved colleagues in several significant ways. They are more likely to describe their jobs more stimulating or higher in range of job characteristics, including variety, autonomy, task identity and feedback (Elloy et al., 1991).

Adoption of the Job Involvement Inventory

The Job Involvement Inventory developed by Dr. Rama Mohan Babu (1992) was adopted for the purpose of the present study. The Inventory consists 20 items. It is a five point attitude scale with alternatives, *Strongly Agree, Agree, Doubtful, Disagree, Strongly Disagree.* This inventory is translated into Telugu by the investigator with the help of the experts in the field and is used for the present investigation. The scoring procedure for the job involvement inventory is similar as is followed in Job satisfaction inventory.

Validity

The criterion validity, content validity, intrinsic validity, Face validity and construct validity of the job involvement inventory were established by Dr. Rama Mohan Babu (1992).

Reliability

Reliability can be defined the degree of consistency between two measures of the same thing. Several methods are used to estimate reliability. The more common ones reported in the test manuals are:

1. Measures of stability (Test-Retest)
2. Measures of equivalence
3. Measures of internal consistency
4. Split-half method
5. Kurdar-Richardson's estimates.

In this study measures of stability is measured through. Test-retest-method. The procedure suggested by Garrett (1973) is employed. The correlation coefficient with a sample of 200 is 0.9352. The internal consistency is also measured threw split-half method. The procedure suggested by Garrett (1973) is employed. The correlation coefficient for the half test with a sample of 300 is 0.8532. The correlation coefficient for the full test also calculated, it is equal to 0.9208. It shows that the Reliability of the Job involvement inventory is very high.

Final Study

The Final Study inventory consists of 20 items. There are 14 Positive items and 6 Negative items in this inventory. Both Telugu and English version of the job involvement inventory were used for the present investigation.

The English version of the job involvement inventory is shown in Appendix -E.

Telugu version of the job involvement inventory is shown in Appendix -F.

Self Concept Scale (SCS)

An idea of the self constructed from the beliefs one holds about oneself and the responses of others.

Self-Concept

The self-concept is a theoretical construct, which allows the integration of all areas of social and emotional development of an individual into a single system. It has been variously defined as "the self as known to the self" (Murphy, 1947) and "those aspects of the individual which seem most vital and important to the person" (Jersield, 1960).

An infant doesn't bring self-concept with him/her at the time of birth. She develops it as a result of her experience. Children acquire it by means of incidental or accidental learning. A child depends heavily on others relation to her for clues about her worth. A child is quite unable to obscrve herself objectively. She is unable to make objective comparisons between herself and other children of the same age group. Some children are nourished in such a manner that effectively communicates to them that they are worthy of love and respect, while other children have entirely different experience. In the process of learning from interaction with others the child not only develops self-concept but also develops an ideal towards which is to strive. Thus self-concept is a key variable in behavior.

In psychological discussion the world "Self" has been used in many ways. Two chief meanings emerge, however, the self as the subject or agent and the self as the individual who is known to himself. The term self-concept has come into common use to refer to the second meaning which refers to the phenomenological approach.

"How a person sees himself (e.g. Competent, amusing, homely, etc.,) this may differ from other people's views to him though it will have been influenced by them (Derek Rowntree, 1981).

1. An individual's perception of self.
2. A psychological contract that is more complex than implied or assumed by most educators (D.R. Singh, 2002) self-concept refers to the pictures or images a

person has of himself (R.P. Taneja, 1991 and A term of Experts, 2003).

Adoption of the Self-Concept Scale

The self-concept scale developed by Dr. (Miss) Mukta Rani Rastogi (1974) was adopted for the purpose of the present study. This scale consists of 51 items divided into 10 areas. It is five-point attitude scale with alternatives *Strongly Agree, Agree, Undecided, Disagree* and *Strongly Disagree.* The 10 areas are:

1. Health and Sex appropriateness
2. Abilities
3. Self-confidence
4. Self-acceptance
5. Worthiness
6. Present, Past and Future
7. Beliefs and Convictions
8. Feeling of shame and guilt
9. Sociability
10. Emotional maturity

This scale is translated into Telugu with the help of the experts and is used in the present investigation. The item numbers each area of the self-concept scale are presented in Table 4.4.

Scoring Procedure for the Self-concept

In the self-concept scale, 5 alternative answers are given to each question. The students are directed to read the instructions at the beginning. The students were motivated to give only one answer for each question. The investigator also tried to make them understand. After collecting the answer sheets the scoring was done with the help of answer key. The total raw score of each testee was marked on the top of the answer sheet.

Table 4.4

The item numbers in each area of the Self-concept scale

Sl.No.	Description	Item Numbers
1.	Health and Sex appropriateness	6 20 29 32 34 & 46 P P N N P & P
2.	Abilities	4 8 12 23 36 38 39 & 42 P P N N P N N & P
3.	Self-confidence	7 9 14 16 & 44 P P N N & P
4.	Self-acceptance	2 10 17 & 35 P N N & N
5.	Worthiness	1 3 19 25 27 41 & 48 P N N P P N & P
6.	Present, Past and Future	18 22 26 31 & 40 P P N N & P
7.	Belief and convictions	24 47 & 49 N P & P
8.	Feeling of same and guilt	5 13 28 30 & 50 N N N N & N
9.	Sociability	33 37 43 & 45 N P P & N
10.	Emotional maturity	11 15 21 & 51 N N N & N

Note: The letters 'P' or 'N' below each item show the Positiveness or Negativeness of the items.

Validity

The validity of a test or scale refers to its accuracy. Dr. (Miss) Mukta Rani Rastogi (1974) established

(*i*) Criterion Validity

(*ii*) Content Validity

(*iii*) Construct Validity of the self-concept scale

Reliability

Reliability can be defined as the degree of consistency between two measures of the same inventory. There are several methods to estimate the reliability of a test. The more common ones reported in the test manuals are:

1. Measures of stability (Test-Retest)
2. Measures of equivalence
3. Measures of internal consistency
4. Split-half method
5. Kurdar–Richard son's estimates.

In this method internal consistency is measured through split-half method. The procedure suggested by Garrett (1973) is employed. The correlation coefficient for the half test with a sample of 200 is 0.8541. The correlation coefficient for the full test is also calculated. It is equal to 0.9213 and it shows that the reliability of instruments is very high.

Final Study

The Final Study inventory consists of 51 items. There are 23 Positive items and 28 Negative items in this inventory. Telugu version of self-concept inventory was used for the present investigation.

The English version of final self-concept inventory is shown in Appendix-G.

The Telugu version of self-concept inventory is shown in Appendix–H.

Cattell's Personality Questionnaire (Form 'C')

The present investigator search for the theories of personality and the means of measuring it which account for the totality of behavior. Cattell's theory, of all the numerous theories, is the only theory based on the principle of totality behaviour of the individual. Before describing the 16 personality factor questionnaire, it is appropriate to discuss the nature of personality to know how the 16 personality factor questionnaire measures the total personality of the individual.

The Nature of the Personality

There are so many definitions about personality. In order to know the nature of personality some important definitions are discussed hereunder.

Some define personality as, "one's social stimulus value". Other define it as, "The sum total of innate depositions, impulses, appetites, instincts, tendencies and habits". Another type of definition say that, "personality is more than the sum of its parts, and that 'more than' is its pattern of organization". Some people define personality as "An individual's characteristics pattern of adjustment".

According to Cattell (1950), "Personality is that which permits a prediction of what a person will do in a given situation". His theory is based on personality sphere concept (Cattell, 1946, 1957, 1994)—a design to ensure initial item coverage for all the behaviour that commonly enters rating and the dictionary description of personality. It focuses heavily on "source traits". Cattell defines source traits as the spring of the human behaviour. Much is becoming known about the nature of these dimensions through studies with ratings, with laboratory measures, and with real life situations (Buros, 1965; Cattell, 1965; Cattell and Morony, 1962; Cattell and Scheier, 1965, Cattell, 1956; Cattell and Stice, 1954; Laird and Laird, 1951; Ostfield et al., 1964; Hall and Lindzey, 1957). According to him, a trait of any variety is a mental structure which is relatively fixed characteristic of the individual, functioning from time to time in behaviour.

Guilford (1959) defined personality as, "An individual's personality is his unique pattern of traits. A trait is any distinguishable, relatively enduring way in which an individual differs from another".

While accepting the above definition, it is necessary to understood what a trait is and how traits measures personality.

Personality Traits

Allport (1959) says that, "... a trait is a form of readiness for response... is individually distinctive of its prosessor... guides the course of behaviour and often becomes dynamic and compulsive as well... bio-physical in nature combining in any proportion the fruits of heredity and the fruits of learning". He further says that, "... trait as a generalized and focalized neuro-psychic system (peculiar to the individual), with capacity to render stimuli functionally equivalent, and to initiate and guide consistent (equivalent) forms of adaptative and expressive behaviour".

According to Vemon (1953), "Traits refers to any characteristic in which people differ or vary from one another... they (personality traits) are more general qualities of social and emotional behaviour, the common features which we abstract from observing how people differ".

Cattell (1950), while defining personality as that which permits a prediction of what a person will do in a given situation, says that for his prediction, traits and types are necessary. Discussing about traits he said, that surface traits are the collection of trait elements (cluster) which correlates positively in every possible internal combination and this collection is called a syndrome of surface trait. He further clarifies that by factor analyzing the trait elements (sub-tests relating to trait elements), we can arrive at source traits which are the sources of surface traits.

By factor analysis Cattell arrive at 16 personality factors (source traits), which mostly cover the individuals entire personality in measurable traits. He prepared the 16 personality factor questionnaire for this purpose.

Teachers, to be successful in their profession have to teach effectively in the classroom. The classroom climate is socio-emotional in nature (as Flanders and other people called it). The teacher has to work this socio-emotional climate and he must adjust or adapt for it. Hence, the teacher's behaviour becomes socio-emotional or we may call it as 'psycho-sociological'. This socio-emotional or psycho-social behaviour of individuals, as Vernon stated, can be measured by traits of personality. As Allport stated trait is to initiate and guide consistent forms of adaptative and expressive behaviour. In order to measure personality of teachers in a socio-emotional climate of classroom, the trait theory, which tells about the general quality of social and emotional behaviour of individuals is accepted in the present investigation and to assess the personality of teachers 16 personality factor questionnaire of Cattell's is selected as a tool.

Concepts Relating to Personality Characteristics

The study of personality covers a varied and complex domain. It seeks to discover the reasons for a wide range of human behaviours to account for their occurrence, and to assess their roles in the total person (Gordon, 1966). According to Gordon (1966), there are some qualities of human behaviour which are as follows:

1. *Enduring Characteristics:* Personality includes the enduring characteristics of the drives and traits which modulate the individual's behaviour throughout his life.
2. *Unique Characteristics:* No two individuals are alike. They differ in the intensity of the drives and motives.
3. *Lifestyle:* It differs to the manner in which individual does what he does. The lifestyle aspect of personality requires us to pay particular attention to those traits that describe an individual's customary ways of doing things as well as the things he likely to do and avoid doing.
4. *Behavioural Organisation:* Most people in a society have about the same motive and traits, but they tend to differ considerably in the relative strength of the motives and traits they share. It is for this reason

that psychologists are interested in the organization of behaviours within a person. The organizational aspect of personality is most clearly indicated by psychographs.

Some Glaring Facts Regarding Personality

After observing the number of definitions given by various authors, Mangal (1983) concluded the following facts about personality.

1. Firstly, the personality is something unique and specific. Everyone of us is a unique pattern in ourselves. No two individuals not even the identical twins behave in precisely the same way over any period of time. Everyone of us has specific characteristics for making adjustments.
2. The second main characteristics of personality is self-consciousness. The man is described as a person or to have a personality when the idea of self enters into his consciousness. We do not attribute personality to a dog and even a child cannot be described as a personality because it has only a vague sense of personal identity.
3. Personality includes everything about a person. It is all that a person has about him. It included all the behaviour patterns, i.e., conative, cognitive and affective and covers not only the conscious activities but goes deeper to semi-conscious and unconscious also.
4. It is not just a collection of so many traits or characteristics which is known as personality. By counting the bricks only how can we describe the wall of a house? It needs something more and actually personality is more than this. It is an organization of some psycho-physical system or some behaviour characteristics and functions as a unified whole. Just as to tell what an elephant is, we can not say that it

is like a pillar only by examining its legs. In the same way by looking through one's physique sociability we cannot pass judgment over one's personality. It is only when we go carefully in all the aspects—biological as well as social—we can make an idea about his personality.

5. Personality is not static. It is dynamic and even in process of change and modification. As we have said earlier that personality is all that a person has about him. It gives him all that I needed for his unique adjustment in his environment. The process of making adjustment to environment is continuous. One has to struggle with the environment as well as the inner forces throughout the span of his life. As a result one has to bring modification and change in one's personality patterns and it makes the nature of personality dynamic instead static one.
6. Every personality is the product of heredity and environment. Both contribute significantly towards the development of the child's personality.
7. Learning and acquisition of experiences contribute towards growth and development of personality. Every personality is the end product of this process of learning and acquisition.
8. Every person's personality has one more distinguishing feature that is, aiming to an end towards some specific goals. Man's personality can be judged through a study and interpretation of the goals he has set for himself to achieve and the approaches he makes to the personality of an individual by calling it by the name, 'life style of an individual'.

Indeed this short and concise explanation of the term, has a wide meaning. It draws a beautiful portrait of an individual's totality. It may be understood to mean as the sum total of one's way of behaving towards oneself and others as well. It also predicts one's nature of behaviour as how one will behave in a particular situation and one's pattern of adjustment to the ever-changing forces of environment.

Selection of the Tool

It is obvious that selection of a tool for measuring personality poses serious problems. In this connection it may also be noted that the problems of justification of the choice looms large. One may cut a sorry figure in explaining for choice. This situation can be solved if we study the theory behind a particular tool and the rationale with which it was prepared. The selection of Cattell's 16 PF test in the present research was also not arbitrary and has been made after lot of deliberations and study of theory which has been supported amply by Stern (1921) and Allport (1937) in following works.

Stern observes as: "We have the right and obligation to develop a concept of trait as a definitive doctrine, for in all activity of the person, there is besides a variable portion, likewise a constant purposive portion, and this later we isolate as a concept of trait".

Allport's contention is equally forceful. He asserts that, "Traits are discovered not be deductive reasoning, not by faith, not by naming, and are themselves never directly observed. They are observed only through an inference made necessary by the demonstrable consistency of the separate observable acts of behaviour.

Vernon (1963) says that a person's behaviour in any situation depends, of course, on specific features of that situation and on his temporary feelings or state of mind, but it depends also on his more enduring characteristics—abilities, habits and more general dispositions which may be called traits.

Cattell (1961) says that source traits, as measured by the 16 PF test, are the spring of human behaviour. He defines personality as "that which permits a prediction of what the person will do in a given situation" (Cattell, 1950). This definition is consist with the contention of Marxi and Hillix (1973) that "the theory of personality is really identical with general theory of behaviour, for Cattell's definition would fit theories of behaviours".

In view of the above theoretical as well as practical considerations Cattell's 16 PF questionnaires was selected. The 16 PF questionnaires is an objectively acceptable test devised by basic research in psychology to give the most complete coverage of personality possible in a brief time. Coverage of personality is insured by the sixteen functionally-independent and psychologically-meaningful dimensions isolated by over twenty years of factor analytical research on normal and clinical groups. Therefore, having a certain position on one, does not prevent the persons having any position whatever on any other. Thus, each of the sixteen scales brings an entirely new piece of information about the person, a condition not found in many alleged multi-dimensional scales.

Moreover, a scoring system is provided whereby, from the sixteen factors, one can extract and work with only four broader (and less specific) traits-anxiety, extraversion, alert poise and independence. Experience with 16 PF in clinical, educational and industrial psychology shows that the use of the 16 traits gives actual prediction.

In view of the above theoretical as well as practical considerations Cattell's 16 PF questionnaires was selected.

Brief Description of 16 Personality Factors

The Cattell's 16 personality factors questionnaire was used to measure the personality of the teachers, in the present investigation. A brief description of each personality factor is given below:

Factor A: Reserved, detached, critical, cool *vs.* Outgoing, Warmhearted, easy-going, participating.

The person who scores low on Factor A 'tends to be stiff, cool, skeptical and alone. He likes things rather than people, working alone, and avoiding clash of view points. He is likely to be 'precise' and 'rigid' in his way of doing things and in personal standards, and in many occupations these are desirable traits. He may tend, at times, to be critical, objective or hard.

The person who scores high on factor 'A' tends to be good natured, easy-going, emotionally expressive, ready to cooperative, attentive to people, soft-hearted; kindly and adoptable. He likes occupations dealing with people and socially impressive situations. He readily forms active groups. He is generous in personal relations, less afraid of criticism and better able to remember the names of the people.

Factor B: Less, intelligent, concrete, thinking *vs*. More intelligent, abstract thinking.

The person scoring low on factor 'B' tends to be slow to learn and grasp, dull and sluggish. He tends to have little capacity for the higher forms of knowledge and to be somewhat boorish. His dullness may be simply a reflection of low intelligence, or it may represent poor functioning due to psychopathology.

The person who scores high on Factor 'B' tends to be quick to grasp ideas, a fast learner and intelligent. There is some correlation, with level of culture, and some with alertness. High score contra indicates deterioration of mental functions of pathological conditions.

Factor C: Affected by feelings, emotionally less stable *vs*. Emotionally stable, calm, mature.

The person who scores low on Factor 'C' tends to be low in frustration, tolerance for unsatisfactory conditions, changeable evading necessary reality demands, neurotically fatigued, worrying, easily annoyed, generally dissatisfied and having neurotic symptoms (Phobias, sleep, disturbances, psychosomatic complaints etc.). Low score on Factory 'C' is common to almost all forms of neurotic and mental disorders.

The person who scores high on Factor 'C' tends to be emotionally mature, stable, calm, realistic about life, unruffled, possessing ego strength, having an integrated philosophy of life and better able to maintain high group morale. Sometimes he may be a person making a resigned adjustment to unsolved emotional problems.

Factor E: Humble, mild, accommodating, i.e., submissive *vs.* Assertive, independent, aggressive i.e., dominance.

The person who scores low on Factor 'E' tends to be dependent, a follower, and to take action which goes along with the group. He is often soft-hearted, expressive and easily upset. This passivity is part of many neurotic syndromes.

The person who scores high on Factor 'E' tends to be assertive, self-assumed, independent-mined and bold in his approach to situations. He may at times be hard, a law to himself, hostile, tough-minded, authoritarian (managing others) and disregards authority.

Factor F: Sober, prudent, serious, i.e., desurgency *vs.* Happy-go-lucky, Gay, enthusiastic, i.e. surgency.

The person who scores low on Factor 'F' tends to be restrained, reticent and introspective. He is sometimes in communicative, pessimistic anxious and considered to be swung. He tends to be a sober and dependable person.

The person who scores high on this trait tends to be cheerful, active, talkative, frank, expressive, quick, alert and imperturbable. He is frequency chosen as an elected leader. He may be impulsive and mercurial.

Factor G: Expedient, evades rules i.e., weaker super-ego strength *vs.* Conscientious, preserving, rule bound i.e., stronger super-ego strength.

The person who scores low on Factor 'G' tends to be unsteady in purpose. He is often casual and lacking in effort for group undertakings and cultural demands. His freedom from group influence may lead to anti-social acts, but at times, make him more effective, while his refusal to be bound by rules causes him to have less somatic upset from stress.

The person who scores high on Factor 'G' tends to be strong in character, preserving, responsible, determined, consistent, painful, energetic, cautious and well-organized. He is usually conscientious or moralistic and he prefer hard working people to witty companions. The inner 'categorical imperative' of this essential super ego (in the psycho-analytical sense) should be distinguished from the superficially similar 'social ideal self' of Q_3 +.

Factor H: Shy, restrained, timid i.e., Threcita, *vs.* Venturesome, socially-bold i.e., Parnia.

The person who scores low on this trait tends to be shy, withdrawing, cautious, retiring, cooling a 'well flower'. He usually has inferiority feelings. He tends to be slow and impeded in speech in expressing himself, dislikes occupations with personal contacts, prefers one or two close friends to large groups, and is not given to keeping in contact with all that is going on around him.

The person who scores high on Factor 'H' tends to be sociable, bold, ready to try new things, spontaneous and abundant in emotional response. His 'thick skinnedness' enables him to face wear and tear in dealing with people and grueling emotional situations without fatigue. However, he can be careless of details, ignore danger signals, and consume much time. He tends to be "pushy" and actively interested in the opposite sex.

Factor I: Touch-mined, self-reliant, i.e., Harria, *vs.* Tender-mined, dependent, sensitive, i.e. Premsia.

The person who scores low on Factor 'I' tends to be practical, realistic, masculine, independent responsible, but skeptical of subjective and 'uncultured'. He is sometimes unmoved, hard, cynical and smug. He tends to keep a group operating on a practical and realistic 'no-nonsense' basis.

The person who scores high on this trait tends to be tender-mined, day-dreaming, artistically, fastidious. He is sometimes demanding of attention and help. He is impatient, dependent and impractical. He dislikes crude people and rough occupations. He tends to slow up group performance, and to upset group morals by unrealistic fussiness.

Factor L: Trusting, adaptable, free of jealousy i.e., Alaxia *vs.* Suspicious, self-opinionated, hard to fool, i.e., Protension.

The person who scores high on Factor 'L' tends to be free of jealous tendencies, adaptable, cheerful, uncompetitive, and concerned about other people and a good team-worker.

The person who scores high on Factor 'L' tends to be mistrusting and doubtful. He is often involved in his own ego, is self-opinionated, and interested in internal mental life. He is usually deliberate in his actions, unconcerned about other people and a poor team member.

Factor M: Practical, careful, conventional i.e., Praxermia *vs.* Imaginative, wrapped up in inner urgencies i.e., Autia.

The person who scores low on Factor 'M' tends to be anxious to do the right things, attentive to practical matters, and subject to the dedications of what is observiously possible. He is concerned over details, able to keep his held in emergencies, but sometimes unimaginative and narrowly correct.

The person who scores high on Factor 'M' tends to be unconventional, unconcerned over matters, bohemian, self-motivated, ego-centric, sensitive and imaginative. He sometimes, makes emotional scenes, is some what irresponsible, impractical and undependable. He is often rejected in group situations.

Factor N: Forthright, natural, artless, i.e., Artlessness *vs.* Shrewed, calculating wordly, i.e., Shredness.

The person who scores low on Factor 'N' tends to be unsophisticated, sentimental and simple. He sometimes crude and awkward, but easily pleased and content with what comes and is natural and spontaneous.

The person who scores high on this trait tends to be polished, experienced, worldly and shrewd. He is often hard-headed and analytical. He is an intellectual and unsentimental approach to situations, an approach akin to cynicism.

Factor O: Placid, Self-assumed, confident i.e., Untroubled adequacy *vs.* Apprehensive, worrying, depressive, troubled i.e., Guilt Proneness.

The person who scores low on Factor 'O' tends to be placed and calm, with unshakable nerve. He has a mature and unanxious confidence in himself and his capacity to deal with things. He is resilient and secure.

The person who scores high on Factor 'O' tends to be depressed, moody, a worrier, suspicious, brooding and avoiding people. He has a child-like tendency to anxiety in difficulties. He does not feel accepted in groups or free to participate. High Factor 'O' score is very common in clinical groups of all types.

Factor Q_1: Conservative, tolerant of traditional difficulties i.e., Conservatism *vs.* Experimenting, critical, free thinking i.e., Radicalism.

The person scores low on Factor 'Q_1' tends to be overly cautious and moderate. He is opposed any change, inclined to go along with traditions, and trends not to be interested in analytical "intellectual" thought.

The person who scores high on Factor 'Q_1' tends to be interested in intellectual matters and has doubts on fundamental issues. He frequently takes issues with ideas, either old or new. He tends to be well informed, less inclined to moralize, more inclined to experiment in life generally and more tolerant in inconvenience and change.

Factor Q_2: Group–dependent, sound followed i.e., Group adherence *vs.* Self-sufficient, resourceful i.e. Self-sufficiency.

The person who scores low on Factor 'Q_2' prefers to work and make decisions with other people and depends on social approval and admiration. He tends to go along with the group and may be lacking in individual resolution. He is not necessary gregarious by choice, rather he needs group support.

The person who scores high on Factor 'Q_2' is temperamentally independent, accustomed to go in his own way, making decisions and taking action on his own. He discounts public opinion, but is not necessarily dominant in his relation with others (see Factor E). He does not dislike people but simply does not mind their agreement or support.

Factor Q_3: Undisciplined, self-conflict, careless i.e., Low integration *vs.* Controlled, socially precise, following self-image. i.e., High self-concept control.

The person who scores low on Factor 'Q_3' will not be bothered with will-control and regard for social demands. He is not over-considerate, careful, on pains-taking. He may feel maladjusted and may show maladjustment.

The person who scores high on Factor 'Q_3' tends to have strong control on his emotions and general behaviour is inclined to be socially aware and careful and evidence what is commonly termed 'self-respect' and regard for social reputation. He sometimes tends, however, to be obstinate. Effective leaders and some paranoids are high on 'Q_3'.

Factor Q_4: Relaxed, tranquil, unfrosted i.e., Low ergic tension *vs.* Tense, frusted, driven i.e., Ergic tension.

The person, who scores low on Factor 'Q_4' tends to be sedate, relaxed, composed and satisfied (not frustrated). In some situations, his over satisfaction can lead to laziness and low performance, in the sense that low motivation produce little trail and error, conversely high tension level may disrupt school and work performance.

The person who scores high on Factor 'Q_4' tends to be tense, excitable, restless, fretful and impatient. He is often fatigued, but unable to remain inactive. In groups he takes a poor view of the degree of unity, orderliness, and leadership.

Adoption of the Instrument

The Cattell's 16-personality factor questionnaire Form-C was adopted as a tool to assess personality of the teachers in the present study. In terms of personality factors measured, Form-C is exactly analysis parallel to Form-A and B. Form-C based on an extensive factor analysis is a good test with maximum reliability and validity possible with only six items per factor. Form-C like Form-A and B, tests as much of the total personality as can be covered by a questionnaire. It gets at such basic independent factors as emotional stability, dominance etc. The 16 personality factors test leaves out no important aspects of total personality. Among personality tests, this is pure a product of factor analysis as can be found. Each item has an appreciable saturation by one of the 16 source traits of ability, temperament and character integration as claimed by the authors. In addition, Form-C has the advantage of ease of administration and scoring. A note may be added about the motivational distortion (MD) scores. In the opinion of Cattell, most questions are designed to be as free as possible of value implications so that the persons will not be tempted to answer on any particular dimension for the sake of social approval. Still the likelihood of distortion in Factor H and Q_2 is recognized and a correction for these factors is suggested. The correction is done by taking away one point from Factor H and to add one to Factor Q_2 if MD score exceeds twelve points (Cattell and Eber, 1962).

Form-C, being shorter in length than A or B, is as effective as Forms A or B. It has an elementary vocabulary which most subjects would follow. The inclusion of index to guard against attempts at distortions of self-picture is an additional advantage. The growing evidence from a number of studies in various fields suggest that the taking into account of all the 16 dimensions of personality gives a better prediction than what may be obtained by a single scale test. In this sense, the 16 personality factor questionnaire is that to be the most suitable for the present investigation.

"The sixteen dimensions or scales are essentially independent. Correlations between one and another are usually negligible. Having a certain position on a dimension does not prevent a person from having any position whatever on another" (Cattell and Eber, 1962).

Moreover, in the 16 personality factor questionnaire, we do not interpret the factors from the nature of the subject's statements about himself, but from the known correlations between these 'mental interiors' as found in questionnaire factors and the factors established in behaviour. In other words, the question responses are treated as behaviour, not as valid self ratings.

Thus, the 16 personality factor test Form-C of 1969 was adopted for the present investigation to assess the personality of the Teacher Educators.

Scoring Procedure for 16 PF (Form 'C')

In the 16 personality factors questionnaire, three alternative answers are given to each question. The subjects are motivated to give only one answer for each question. A preliminary instruction was made to know whether there is more than one answer or not to each question in the answer sheet. Then the answers are scored according to the weightage given by the author. The scoring was done for each individual Teacher Educator and for each factor.

Reliability and Validity

For calculating reliability and validity, the procedure suggested by Garrett (1973) was followed. Reliability of the subtests of each factor (based on raw scores) as obtained by spilt-half technique and validity which is the square root of reliability, are presented in Table 4.5. The spilt half reliability was calculated on a sample of 250.

Table 4.5

Reliability and Validity of 16 PF Form C using spilt-half technique

Factor	A	B	C	E	F	G	H	I
Reliability	0.591	0.620	0.531	0.663	0.649	0.751	0.669	0.689
Validity	0.768	0.787	0.728	0.814	0.805	0.866	0.817	0.830

Factor	L	M	N	O	Q_1	Q_2	Q_3	Q_4
Reliability	0.556	0.569	0.601	0.710	0.701	0.760	0.555	0.686
Validity	0.745	0.754	0.775	0.842	0.837	0.871	0.744	0.828

Retest was also conducted on a sample of 150 with a gap of 15 days. The test-retest reliability and validity for each factor are given in Table 4.6.

Table 4.6

Reliability and Validity of 16 PF Form C using test-retest technique

Factor	A	B	C	E	F	G	H	I
Reliability	0.556	0.628	0.560	0.644	0.620	0.758	0.642	0.678
Validity	0.745	0.792	0.748	0.802	0.787	0.870	0.801	0.823

Factor	L	M	N	O	Q_1	Q_2	Q_3	Q_4
Reliability	0.531	0.582	0.610	0.702	0.715	0.770	0.530	0.670
Validity	0.728	0.762	0.781	0.837	0.845	0.877	0.728	0.818

Final Study

The 16 PF Form C was administered to Five hundred and Ninety-Two Teacher Educators working in B.Ed Colleges.

The scoring was done as per the instructions of the 16 PF (Form 'C') manual.

Socio-Demographic Scale

Socio-demographic scale has defined as the ranking of the individual in terms of his/her material belongings and cultural postings along with the degree of respect, power and influence he/she derives. The investigator prepared the socio-demographic scale and used for the present study. The following aspects are included in the Socio-demographic Scale: 1. Sex, 2. Age, 3. Educational Qualifications, 4. Teaching Experience, 5. Marital Status, 6. Occupation of Spouse, 7. Total Salary per Month, 8. Annual Income, 9. Region, 10. Management, 11. Total members in the family, 12. Religion and 13. Caste.

This scale is referred to the experts in the field and necessary modifications are done.

Both English and Telugu version of socio-demographic scale are given in Appendices L and M.

Scoring of the Items

The items with quantitative measurement were considered separately. The numerical values were assigned according to their weightages for the statistical purposes.

Validity and Reliability

Validity and reliability of the Socio-demographic scale was calculated. It was found that the Socio-demographic scale was highly valid and reliable.

FINAL STUDY

The final study was conducted after the construction, standardization and adoption of the research tools as described in preceding pages.

Sample Design

The investigator in person visited the colleges of education after obtaining the permission of the head of institutions and collected data. The sample for the investigation consisted of 592 Teacher Educators working in B.Ed colleges in Andhra Pradesh. The stratified random sampling was applied in three stages. Geographically Andhra Pradesh State is divided into three regions namely Circar, Telangana, and Rayalaseema. From each region some Government and University Colleges, Private Colleges and Minority Colleges were taken. The Male and Female Teacher Educators working in selected B.Ed Colleges of Education were taken for purpose of this investigation.

The data were collected on 178 Teacher Educators in Circar, 214 in Telangana and 200 Rayalaseema regions. Among 592 Teacher Educators for this study, there were 96 in govt and university colleges, 324 in private colleges and 172 minority colleges. Among 592 Teacher Educators, there were 318 Male and 274 Female Teacher Educators. The sample design for the Final study is presented in Table 4.7.

Table 4.7

Sample Design for final study

Region	Govt.			Private			Minority			Total
	Male	Female	Total	Male	Female	Total	Male	Female	Total	
Circar	22	18	40	49	43	92	26	20	46	178
Telangana	15	15	30	57	58	115	35	34	69	214
Rayalaseema	12	14	26	69	48	117	33	24	57	200
Total	49	47	96	175	149	324	94	78	172	592

Collection of Data

The Heads of the selected colleges in the sample frame were requested to permit the investigator for distributing the questionnaires to the Teacher Educators. All the questionnaires were distributed to each Teacher Educator who was present in the college on the day of visit. The purpose of research and how to fill the questionnaire is explained to the Teacher Educators, and they were requested to return the filled-in questionnaires on the next day. Thus the investigator collected the filled-in questionnaires. If any Teacher Educator did not return the filled in questionnaire the investigator had given the stamped self address envelop and asked the concerned Teacher Educator to send the filled-in questionnaire through postal service. Thus finally the investigator was able to collect the needed research data from 592 Teacher Educators.

Scoring and Analysis

The collected data were scored following the procedures already described. The analysis was carried out on the basis of objectives of the study and hypotheses formulated by employing appropriate statistical techniques. Tables and graphs were prepared wherever necessary to present the data.

Statistical Techniques Employed

Frequency distribution tables were prepared for the Job satisfaction of Teacher Educators wherever necessary. Measures of central tendency, measures of dispersion, skewness, kurtosis, coefficient of variation and standard error of mean were calculated wherever necessary. The significance tests like 't' and 'F' were employed to test different hypotheses. Multiple 'R' was calculated by carrying out the stepwise regression analysis to find out whether it was possible to estimate the Job satisfaction of Teacher Educators. The obtained numerical results were adumbrated by graphical representations.

For Statistical formulae, the following books were referred.

1. *Statistical Analysis in Educational Research* by Lind Quist, F.F., (1940)
2. *Statistical Works for Research Workers* by Fisher (1950)

3. *Fundamentals Statistics in Psychology and Education* by Guilford (1950)
4. *Statistics in Psychology and Education* by Henry E., Garrett and R.S Wood Worth (1961)
5. *Statistics in Education and Psychology* by Yate (1965)
6. *Statistical Principles in Experimental Design* by Edwards (1971)
7. *Experimental Design in Psychological Research* by Edwards (1971)
8. *Statistics in Psychology and Education* by Garrett (1973)
9. *Statistical Methods* by Gupta (1974)
10. *Applied Regression Analysis* by Draper and Smith (1981)
11. *Statistics in Psychology and Education* by Mangal (2002)

CHAPTER 5

ANALYSIS AND INTERPRETATION OF THE DATA

This chapter deals with analysis and interpretation of the data.

The data is presented in the form of:

1. Frequency distribution tables.
2. Factorial designs.
3. 't' values and 'F' ratios with respect to the influence of independent variables on dependent variable.
4. Regression Analysis.

FREQUENCY DISTRIBUTION TABLES

The distribution characteristics for the job satisfaction scores namely Mean (M), Median (Md), Mode (Mo), Range (R), Quartile Deviation (QD), Standard Deviation (SD), Skewness (Sk), Kurtosis (Ku), Coefficient of variation (CV) and Standard Error of Mean (SEM), for the total sample and for various divisions of samples are studied. The Skewness and Kurtosis are used wherever necessary for normal distribution The Value of Skewness is 0.00 and Kurtosis is 3.00. The distribution characteristics are presented and discussed here under.

Total Sample

The investigator measured job satisfaction scores of the Teacher Educators by using the constructed and standardised Job Satisfaction Inventory (JSI) developed by the investigator.

The job satisfaction scores Mean the total score on all the items (80 items) of the job satisfaction inventory. It is an attitude scale with 5 alternatives–*Strongly Agree, Agree, Doubtful, Disagree,* and *Strongly Disagree.* The minimum and maximum scores on job satisfaction inventory are 80 and 400 respectively. The frequency distribution of job satisfaction scores for total sample (N = 592) is presented in Table 5.1.

Table 5.1

Frequency distribution of job satisfaction scores

S.No.	C.I	Limits	Mid point	Frequency	CF	CPF
1.	191-210	190.5-210.5	200.5	10	10	1.68
2.	211-230	210.5-230.5	220.5	74	84	14.18
3.	231-250	230.5-250.5	240.5	84	168	28.37
4.	251-270	250.5-270.5	260.5	114	282	47.63
5.	271-290	270.5-290.5	280.5	142	424	71.62
6.	291-310	290.5-310.5	300.5	77	501	84.62
7.	311-330	310.5-330.5	320.5	54	555	93.75
8.	331-350	330.5-350.5	340.5	28	583	98.47
9.	351-370	350.5-370.5	360.5	8	591	99.83
10.	371-390	370.5-390.5	380.5	1	592	100

Total (N) = 592

Mean (M) = 273.62 | Median (Md) = 273

Mode (Mo) = 271.7635 | Range (R) = 189

Quartile deviation (QD) = 25.5 | Standard Deviation (SD) = 35.7827

Skewness (Sk) = 0.04 | Kurtosis (Ku) = 2.5481

Co-efficient Variance (CV) = 13.0776 | Standard Error of Mean (SEM) = 1.4707

It is observed from Table 5.1, the Mean job satisfaction score is 273.62. There are 80 items in the Job Satisfaction inventory. The neutral value on the job satisfaction inventory is 240 (80 × 3). Hence it is inferred that the Teacher Educators working in B.Ed. colleges have better satisfaction with their jobs, because the Mean job satisfaction score (273.62) is greater than the neutral value (240). The value of Skewness (S_k) and Kurtosis (Ko) are 0.04 and 2.55 respectively. For the normal distribution, the values of Skewness and Kurtosis are 0.00 and 3.00 respectively. Hence the frequency distribution of job satisfaction scores for the total sample is slightly positively skewed and Lepto Kurtic.

Hoppock (1935) study revealed that most of the satisfied teachers lived in such towns with more than 10000 populations. Majority of the Teacher Education institutions are established in such localities only.

According to Davis (1981), the primary sources of satisfaction of teachers were in aspects of working with students, intellectual stimulation, autonomy, holidays, and job security. So the Teacher Educators may satisfy in this state by their autonomy, intellectual stimulation and working with the graduates and postgraduate students. In general there is a opinion among the educationists that teachers are not satisfied but the result proved that they are satisfied with their job. Teacher Educator's, satisfaction with their job is a good sign for development of the system of education in this state.

Satisfied teachers expected to hold their jobs longer, to be able to engage in more responsive, positive and consistent interaction with children, and to influence positively students' performance (Maslach and Leiter, 1999). To get the development of any system one should have the experienced employee in this system. Until and unless we are able to retain the employees for a long time in the system, it is not possible to gain experience and also male Teacher Educator is able to devote more time towards his profession. This is a progressive sign for the growth of the system.

Fenech (2006) reported poor work conditions, low salaries, heavy workloads, unrealistic expectations from managers, low professional status, organizational conflict, and reduced autonomy. Due to NCTE norms there is an improvement in the working conditions of the colleges of education. The salaries of the majority Teacher Educators are very low before 2002. After that there is an improvement in the salary structure of these Teacher Educators with the growth of institutions and demand from the students. But now demand is going down in the private institutions because of unrealistic growth in number. Structured program is prepared by the university authorities for the teacher education program so there is no unrealistic expectation from the management in this area.

The bar diagram for distribution of job satisfaction scores for the total sample is shown in Graph 5.1.

The frequency polygon distribution of job satisfaction for total sample is presented in Graph 5.2.

The ogive curve for the distribution of job satisfaction scores for the total sample is given in Graph 5.3.

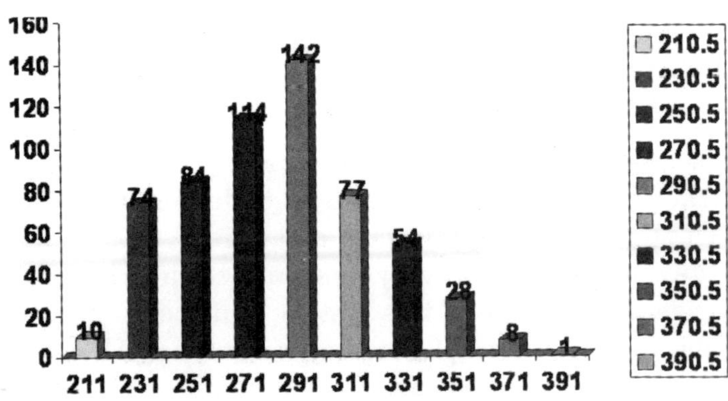

Graph 5.1. The bar diagram for distribution of job satisfaction scores for the total sample

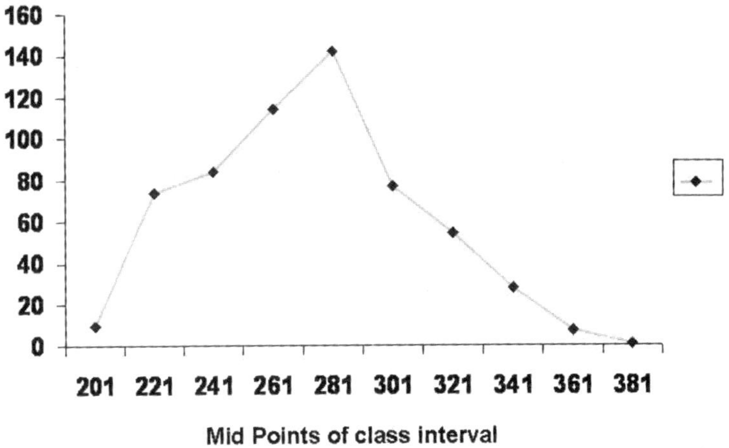

Graph 5.2. The frequency polygon for the distribution of Job Satisfaction Scores for the total sample

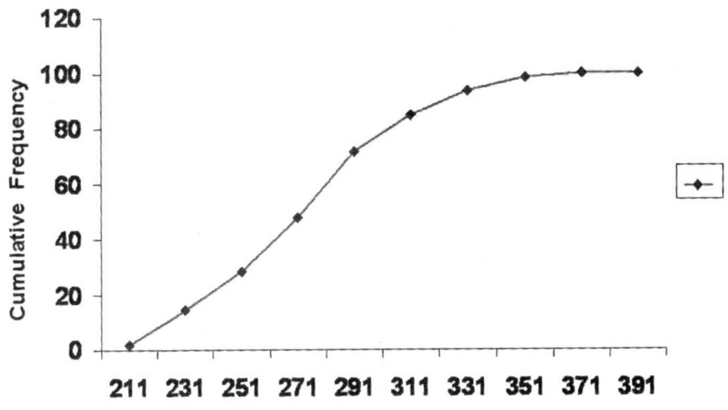

Graph 5.3. The ogive for the distribution of job satisfaction scores for the total sample

Male and Female Teacher Educators

Frequency distribution of Job Satisfaction Scores for Male Teacher Educators (N = 318) is presented in Table 5.2.

Table 5.2

Frequency distribution of job satisfaction scores for the males

Sl. No.	C.I.	Limits	Mid point	Frequency	CF	CPF
1.	191-210	190.5-210.5	200.5	4	4	1.257862
2.	211-230	210.5-230.5	220.5	42	46	14.46541
3.	231-250	230.5-250.5	240.5	45	91	28.61635
4.	251-270	250.5-270.5	260.5	64	155	48.74214
5.	271-290	270.5-290.5	280.5	79	234	73.58491
6.	291-310	290.5-310.5	300.5	35	269	84.59119
7.	311-330	310.5-330.5	320.5	27	296	93.08176
8.	331-350	330.5-350.5	340.5	16	312	98.11321
9.	351-370	350.5-370.5	360.5	6	318	100

Total (N) = 318
Mean (M) = 270.90
Median (Md) = 272
Mode (Mo) = 270.18
Range(R) = 170
Quartile deviation (QD) = 22
Standard deviation (S.D) = 35.38
Skewness (Sk) = 0.08
Kurtosis (Ku) = 2.60
Co-efficient variance (CV) = 12.96
Standard error of mean (SEM) = 1.98

It is seen from Table 5.2 that the Mean Job Satisfaction scores for Male Teacher Educators is 272.90. The neutral value of job satisfaction scores on the job satisfaction inventory is 240 (80 × 3). It indicates that male Teacher Educators have positive job satisfaction. The values of Skewness (Sk), and Kurtosis (Ku) are 0.08 and 2.60 respectively. It is inferred from above values that the frequency distribution of the job satisfaction scores for male Teacher Educators is slightly positively Skewed and Lepto Kurtic. The other distribution characteristics are also given in Table 5.2.

The frequency distribution of job satisfaction scores of Female Teacher Educators (N = 274) is given in Table 5.3.

Table 5.3

Frequency distribution of job satisfaction scores for the Females

Sl. No.	C.I.	Limits	Mid point	Frequency	CF	CPF
1.	191-210	190.5-210.5	200.5	6	6	2.189781
2.	211-230	210.5-230.5	220.5	32	38	13.86861
3.	231-250	230.5-250.5	240.5	39	77	28.10219
4.	251-270	250.5-270.5	260.5	50	127	46.35036
5.	271-290	270.5-290.5	280.5	63	190	69.34307
6.	291-310	290.5-310.5	300.5	42	232	84.67153
7.	311-330	310.5-330.5	320.5	27	259	94.52555
8.	331-350	330.5-350.5	340.5	12	271	98.90511
9.	351-370	350.5-370.5	360.5	2	273	99.63504
10.	371-390	370.5-390.5	380.5	1	274	100

Total (N) = 274

Mean (M) = 274.44

Mode (Mo) = 276.1

Quartile deviation (QD) = 27

Skewness (Sk) = 0.0093

Co-efficient variance (CV) = 13.19

Median (Md) =275

Range (R) = 189

Standard deviation (SD) = 36.22

Kurtosis (Ku) = 2.50

Standard error of mean (SEM) = 2.18

It is observed from Table 5.3 that the Mean Job Satisfaction scores for Female Teacher Educators are 274.44. It indicates that female Teacher Educators have positive job satisfaction. The values of Skewness and Kurtosis are 0.01 and 2.50 respectively. Hence the frequency distribution of job satisfaction scores for female Teacher Educators is slightly positively Skewed and Lepto Kurtic.

In a study on 240 secondary school teachers, Venkatarami Reddy and Krishna Reddy (1978) found that women teachers were more satisfied than men teachers. Venkatarami Reddy and Babjan (1980); and Venkatarami Reddy and Ramakrishnaiah (1981) also obtained similar results. This study also proved the same.

Bar diagram from the means of job satisfaction of male and female Teacher Educators shown in Graph 5.4.

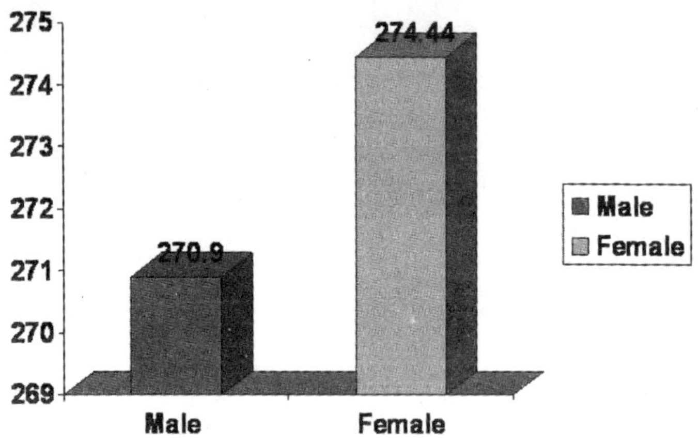

Graph 5.4. Bar diagram from the means of job satisfaction scores of male and female Teacher Educators

Region

The frequency distribution of job satisfaction scores of Teacher Educators working in different regions, namely Rayalaseema, Telangana and Circar, is studied separately. The frequency distribution of job satisfaction scores for Rayalaseema region Teacher Educators is presented in Table 5.4.

It, is observed from Table 5.4 that the Mean job satisfaction scores for Rayalaseema Teacher Educators is 273.3. This value is greater than the neutral value ($80 \times 3 = 240$). Hence, the Rayalaseema Teacher Educators have positive job satisfaction. The values of Skewness and

Kurtosis are 0.03 and 2.62 respectively. The frequency distribution of job satisfaction scores of Rayalaseema Teacher Educators is slightly positively skewed and lepto kurtic and is very closed to normal distribution.

Table 5.4

Frequency distribution of job satisfaction scores for the Rayalaseema region Teacher Educators

S No	C.I	Limits	Mid point	Frequency	CF	CPF
1	191-210	190.5-210.5	200.5	2	2	1
2	211-230	210.5-230.5	220.5	22	24	12
3	231-250	230.5-250.5	240.5	31	55	27.5
4	251-270	250.5-270.5	260.5	39	94	47
5	271-290	270.5-290.5	280.5	52	146	73
6	291-310	290.5-310.5	300.5	29	175	87.5
7	311-330	310.5-330.5	320.5	14	189	94.5
8	331-350	330.5-350.5	340.5	8	197	98.5
9	351-370	350.5-370.5	360.5	3	200	100

Total (N) = 200

Mean (M) = 273.30

Mode (Mo) = 272.40

Quartile deviation (QD) = 23

Skewness (Sk) = 0.03

Co-efficient variance (CV) = 12.45

Median (Md) = 273

Range(R) = 170

Standard deviation (S.D) = 34.02

Kurtosis (Ku) = 2.62

Standard error of mean (SEM) = 2.40

The frequency distribution of job satisfaction scores for Telangana region Teacher Educators is shown in Table 5.5.

It is observed from Table 5.5 that the mean job satisfaction scores for Telangana Teacher Educators is 273.02. It is inferred that the Telangana Teacher Educators have positive job satisfaction. The value of Skewness and Kurtosis are 0.01 and 2.33 respectively. Hence, the frequency distribution of job satisfaction scores of Telangana Teacher

Educators is slightly positively skewed and lepto kurtic. It implies that scores are massed at the low end of the scale, and are spread out gradually toward the high or right end of the scale.

Table 5.5

Frequency distribution of job satisfaction scores for the Telangana region Teacher Educators

Sl.No.	C.I	Limits	Mid point	Frequency	CF	CPF
1.	191-210	190.5-210.5	200.5	6	6	2.803738
2.	211-230	210.5-230.5	220.5	28	34	15.88785
3.	231-250	230.5-250.5	240.5	32	66	30.84112
4.	251-270	250.5-270.5	260.5	39	105	49.06542
5.	271-290	270.5-290.5	280.5	46	151	70.56075
6.	291-310	290.5-310.5	300.5	26	177	82.71028
7.	311-330	310.5-330.5	320.5	22	199	92.99065
8.	331-350	330.5-350.5	340.5	13	212	99.06542
9.	351-370	350.5-370.5	360.5	2	214	100

Total (N) = 214
Mean (M) = 273.02
Mode (Mo) = 275.94
Quartile deviation (QD) = 27
Skewness (Sk) = 0.01
Co-efficient variance (CV) = 13.54

Median (Md) = 274
Range(R) = 167
Standard deviation (SD) = 37.11
Kurtosis (Ku) = 2.233
Standard error of mean (SEM) = 2.53

The frequency distribution of job satisfaction scores for Circar Teacher Educators is given in Table 5.6.

It is clear from Table 5.6 that the mean job satisfaction score for Circar Teacher Educators is 274.68. It indicates that the Circar Teacher Educators have positive job satisfaction. The values of Skewness and Kurtosis are 0.10 and 2.69 respectively. Hence the distribution is slightly positively skeweed and lepto kurtic. It implies that the scores are massed at the low end of the scale and are spread out gradually toward the high or right end of the scale.

Table 5.6

Frequency distribution of job satisfaction scores for the Circar region Teacher Educators

Sl.No.	C.I	Limits	Mid point	Frequency	CF	CPF
1.	191-210	190.5-210.5	200.5	2	2	1.123596
2.	211-230	210.5-230.5	220.5	24	26	14.60674
3.	231-250	230.5-250.5	240.5	21	47	26.40449
4.	251-270	250.5-270.5	260.5	36	83	46.62921
5.	271-290	270.5-290.5	280.5	44	127	71.34831
6.	291-310	290.5-310.5	300.5	22	149	83.70787
7.	311-330	310.5-330.5	320.5	18	167	93.82022
8.	331-350	330.5-350.5	340.5	7	174	97.75281
9.	351-370	350.5-370.5	360.5	3	177	99.4382
10.	371-390	370.5-390.5	380.5	1	178	100

Total (N) = 178

Mean (M) = 274.68 | Median (Md) = 273

Mode (Mo) = 269.62 | Range(R) = 188

Quartile deviation (QD) = 25.50 | Standard deviation (S.D) = 36.04

Skewness (Sk) = 0.10 | Kurtosis (Ku) = 2.69

Co-efficient variance (CV) = 13.12 | Standard error of mean (SEM) = 2.70

The bar diagram for the means of job satisfaction scores of Rayalaseema, Telangana and Circar region Teacher Educators is given in Graph 5.5.

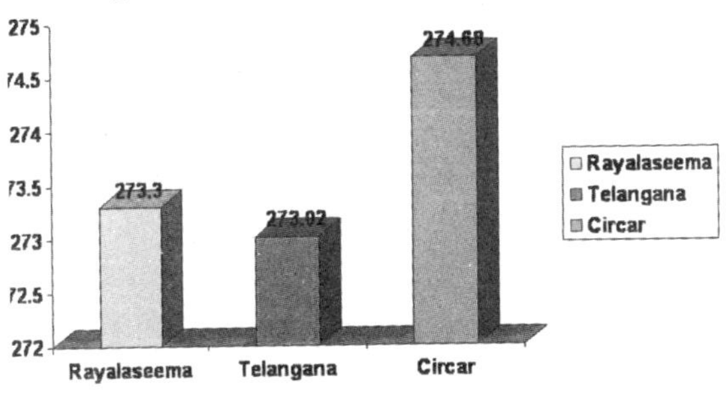

Graph 5.5. The Bar diagram for the means of job satisfaction scores of Rayalaseema, Telangana and Circar Teacher Educators

Composition of Distribution Characteristics of Job Satisfaction Scores

The values of N, M, SD, SK and Ku for all the groups of Teacher Educators on job satisfaction scores are presented in Table 5.7.

Table 5.7

The values of N, M, SD, Sk, and Ku for all groups of Teacher Educators on job satisfaction

Sl.No.	Group	N	M	SD	Sk	Ku
1.	Whole group	592	273.61	35.78	0.04	2.54
2.	Male	318	272.90	35.38	0.08	2.60
3.	Female	274	274.44	36.22	0.0093	2.50
4.	Rayalaseema region	200	273.30	34.02	0.03	2.62
5.	Telangana region	214	273.02	37.11	0.01	2.33
6.	Circar region	178	274.68	36.04	0.10	2.69

Among all the groups the mean job satisfaction score for Circar region Teacher Educators is 274.68 which is the highest among all the groups. The mean job satisfaction score for male Teacher Educators is 272.90 which is the lowest among all the values. It is inferred that Circar region Teacher Educators have better job satisfaction and male Teacher Educators have the lowest job satisfaction among the all the groups.

The Standard Deviation of job satisfaction scores for Telangana region Teacher Educators is 37.11 which is the highest among all the values. It is inferred that the dispassion of job satisfaction scores is more in Telangana region Teacher Educators. The Standard Deviation of job satisfaction scores of Rayalaseema region Teacher Educators is 34.02, which is the least among all the values. Hence, the dispersion of job satisfaction scores of Rayalaseema region Teacher Educators is least among all the groups.

It is observed from Table 5.7 that the values of Skewness for all the groups are positive and are very low. Therefore, the distribution of job satisfaction scores for the most of the groups are very near to normal distribution.

The magnitudes of Kurtosis for all the groups are slightly lower than the normal distribution value. Hence, the distribution of job satisfaction scores for all the groups are slightly lepto kurtic.

FACTORIAL DESIGN

The influence of Sex and Region on job satisfaction scores of Teacher Educators is investigated. 2 x 3 factorial design is employed and results are presented in Table 5.8.

Table 5.8

Results of ANOVA of 2×3 Factorial Design for the job satisfaction score

Sl.No.	Source of Variance	Sum of squares	Degrees of Freedom	Mean Square	'F' Value	Level of significance
1.	A	595.1766	1	595.1766	0.4635	@
2.	B	501.0415	2	250.5208	0.1951	@
3.	AB	4955.7560	2	2477.8780	1.9296	@
4.	Error	752498.5000	586	1284.1270	-	-
	Total	758550.4741	591	-	-	-

Factor A = Sex (2 levels) Factor B = Region (3 levels)

The following Hypotheses are formulated.

Hypothesis 1

There would be no significant influence of the main effects of variables viz., Sex and Region on job satisfaction scores of the Teacher Educators.

Hypothesis 2

There would be no significant interaction effects of the variables viz., Sex and Region on job satisfaction scores of the Teacher Educators.

To test the above Hypotheses, Analysis of variance

(ANOVA) technique is employed using 2 × 3 factorial design and the results are presented in Table 5.8.

It is clear from Table 5.8 that the main effects Sex and Region do not have significant influence on job satisfaction of the Teacher Educators at 0.05 level. The critical or table value of 'F' for 1 and 586 df at 0.05 level is 3.86 and at 0.01 level is 6.69. The critical or Table Value of 'F' for 2 and 586 df at 0.05 level is 3.01 and at 0.01 level is 4.65. Hence, Hypothesis 1 is accepted for the main effects Sex and Region at 0.05 level of significance.

The two factor interaction effort namely Sex × Region does not have significant influence on job satisfaction scores of Teacher Educators at 0.05 level. Hence Hypothesis-2 is accepted for the interaction effects Sex × Region at 0.05 level of significance.

Therefore, it is concluded that the main effects namely Sex and Region and the interaction effect namely Sex × Region have no significant influence on job satisfaction of Teacher Educators.

INFLUENCE OF SOCIO-DEMOGRAPHIC VARIABLES

The influence of socio-demographic variables namely 1. Age, 2. Educational Qualifications, 3. Teacher experience, 4. Marital status, 5. Occupation of the spouse, 6. Salary, 7. Annual income, 8. Management, 9. Total member in the family, 10. Religion and 11. Caste on job satisfaction of Teacher Educators is investigated and the results are presented in the following tables. The following hypothesis is formulated.

Hypothesis 3

There would be no significant influence of socio-demographic variables on job satisfaction of Teacher Educators.

The above hypothesis is tested employing 't' and 'F' techniques wherever applicable.

Richard and Dewhirst (1979) disclosed that age demonstrated a significant positive relationship with extrinsic satisfaction and there was no such relationship between age and intrinsic satisfaction.

Teachers with master or higher degrees were more critical of the professional environment (Smith, 1982). AI-Khaldi (1983) found that employees with higher educational levels were less satisfied with their salary than those with lower education levels.

Venkatarami Reddy and Krishna Reddy (1978), and Ramakrishnaiah (1980) reported no relationship between the two variables, while Butler (1961) found that unmarried beginning teachers were more satisfied than their married counterparts.

However, Inlow (1951), NEA (1957) and Venkatarami Reddy and Babjan (1980) found that married teachers were more satisfied. Sinha and Nair (1965) and Chen (1977) also obtained similar results on factory workers.

It is very unfortunate that the scales of pay of teachers are lower than other categories of employees who possess similar or even lower qualifications, experience and responsibilities, observed by Perumal (1969). He added that such a disparity promotes an unhealthy and undesirable competition and as a result, teachers become a disgusted and a dissatisfied lot.

These findings are supporting the hypothesis that there is no significant effect on job satisfaction.

Age

On the basis of age, the Teacher Educators are divided into two groups namely group 1 (25 to 40 year age) and group 2 (41 to 65 year age). The influence of age on job satisfaction is studied by employing 't' technique and the results are presented in Table 5.9.

It is evident from Table 5.9 that the computed value of 't' (0.92) is less than the critical or table value (1.96) at 0.05

level of significance. Hence, hypothesis 3 is accepted. It is conducted that age has no significant influence on job satisfaction of Teacher Educators.

Table 5.9

Influence of age on job satisfaction

Sl. No.	Age	Number of observations	Mean	SD	't' value	Level of significance
1.	25 to 40	384	272.61	34.44	0.92	@
2.	41 to 65	208	275.46	38.21		

Sajili (1995) reported that job satisfaction increased up to 45 years of age and then declined in the terminal period of 45-65 years among the lecturers in different institutions in Uttar Pradesh. Tripri (1999) revealed that the most satisfied teachers to be older and teaching in the middle school. Similar results were obtained by Shekah (2003). Aajana (2005) in her study observed that teachers over 55 years of age and under 25 were the most-satisfied. Srenivasan (2007) observed that high age groups have more job satisfaction than low age groups.

Educational Qualifications

On the basis of educational qualifications the Teacher Educators are divided into two groups, namely group 1 with Postgraduation (P.G) plus M.Ed., and group 2 with P.G plus M.Ed., plus M.Phil/Ph.D. The influences of educational qualifications of Teacher Educators on job satisfaction is investigated by employing 't'-technique and the results are presented in Table 5.10.

It is observed from Table 5.10 that the computed value of 't' is 1.33 which is less than critical or table value that is 1.96 for 590 df at 0.05 level of significance. Therefore, hypothesis 3 is accepted at 0.05 level of significance. Hence it is concluded that educational qualifications of Teacher Educators do not have significant influence on job satisfaction.

Table 5.10

Influence of educational qualifications on job satisfaction

S.No.	Educational qualifications	Number of observations	Mean	SD	't' values	Level of significance
1.	PG + M.Ed	375	272.13	35.88	1.33	@
2.	PG + M.Ed + Mphil / Ph.D	217	276.18	35.62		

Happock (1935), Sinha and Sarma (1962), Anand (1972), Weaver (1974), and Bernard and Kulandaivel (1976) concluded that there was no relationship between level of education and job satisfaction among employees of various occupations. Here the result is accepting the past research.

Teaching Experience

Based on the Teaching Experience, the Teacher Educators are divided into three groups.

Group 1 is formed with teaching experience up to 5 years.

Group 2 is formed with teaching experience of 6 to 10 years

Group 3 is formed with teaching experience of 11 and above Years.

The influence of teaching experience on job satisfaction of Teacher Educators is investigated by employing one way analysis of variance (ANOVA) and the results are presented in Table 5.11.

Table 5.11

Influence of teaching experience on job satisfaction

S.No.	Teaching experience	Number of observations	Mean	SD	'F' value	Level of significance
1.	Up to 5 years	336	271.99	35.44	2.63	@
2.	6 to 10 years	199	273.47	35.43		
3.	11 and above	57	283.71	38.17		

It is evident from Table 5.11 that the computed value of 'F' is 2.63 which is less than critical or table value (3.01) for

2 and 589 df at 0.05 level of significance. Hence hypothesis 3 is accepted at 0.05 level of significance. Therefore, it is concluded that teaching experience does not have significant influence on the job satisfaction of Teacher Educators.

Weinroth (1977) indicated that experienced teachers, over 55 years of age, with older children, had lower motivation and higher job satisfaction in the intrinsic area compared to one, the young, childless inexperienced teachers, and two, older, experienced teachers with school aged children. Young inexperienced teachers with pre-school children wanted less work pressure and were less satisfied with the amount of pressure on the job than older, experienced teachers with school aged children. Lewis (1982) also found that teachers who had continuous experience in the current school were more satisfied that others.

Marital Status

Based on the marital status, the Teacher Educators are divided into two groups. Group 1 is formed with unmarried Teacher Educators. Group 2 is formed with married Teacher Educators. The impact of marital status on job satisfaction of Teacher Educators is studied by employing 't' technique and the results are shown in Table 5.12.

Table 5.12

Influence of marital status on job satisfaction

S.I No.	Marital status	Number of observations	Mean	SD	't' values	Level of significance
1.	Unmarried	135	272.70	36.35	0.34	@
2.	Married	457	273.88	35.68		

It is observed from Table 5.12 that the computed value of 't' is 0.34 which is less than the critical or table value (1.96) for 590 df at 0.05 level of significance. Therefore, hypothesis 3 is accepted at 0.05 level of significance. Hence it is concluded that the marital status of Teacher Educators does not have significant influence on their job satisfaction.

Jalaja (2004) found again that married teachers seem to be more satisfied with their teaching positions than unmarried teachers.

Neelakandan and Rajendran (2007) found that married employees will have higher job satisfaction than unmarried employees. The result is in agreement to finding of Bhatt (1999) and Bilgic Reyham (1998).

Occupation of Spouse

The influence of occupation of spouse on the job satisfaction of Teacher Educator is investigated. Based on the occupation of spouse, the Teacher Educators are divided into two groups. Group 1 is formed with spouse unemployed. Group 2 formed with spouse employed. t-technique is employed and the results are presented in Table 5.13.

Table 5.13

Influence of occupation of the spouse on job satisfaction

Sl. No.	Occupation of spouse	Number of observations	Mean	SD	't' value	Level of significance
1.	Un employed	288	272.53	35.96	0.71	@
2.	Employed	304	274.64	35.69		

It is clear from Table 5.13 that the computed value of 't' is 0.71. It is for less than the critical or table value (1.96) for 590 df at 0.05 level of significance. Therefore hypothesis-3 is accepted. Hence it is concluded that the marital status of spouse does not have significant bearing on job satisfaction of the Teacher Educators.

Salary

The effect of salary per month on job satisfaction of Teacher Educators is studied. On the basis of monthly salary; the Teacher Educators are divided into three groups. Group 1 formed with Teacher Educators drawing monthly salary up to Rs. 7500. Group-2 is formed with Teacher Educators drawing monthly salary from Rs.7501 to Rs. 15000. Group 3 is formed with Teacher Educators drawing monthly salary from Rs. 15001 and above. One way ANOVA is employed, the results are shown in Table 5.14.

Table 5.14

Influence of salary on job satisfaction

S.No.	Salary (Rs.)	Number of observations	Mean	SD	'F' values	Level of significance
1	Below to 7500	127	271.13	33.34	2.94	@
2	7501 to 15000	395	272.72	35.21		
3	15001 and above	70	283.17	41.98		

It is observed from Table 5.14 that the computed value of 'F' is 2.94. The critical or table value of 'F' for 2 and 589 df at 0.05 level is 3.01. The computed value is less than the table value. Therefore, hypothesis-3 is accepted at 0.05 level of significance. Hence it is concluded that the salary of the Teacher Educators does not have significant effect on their job satisfaction.

Roger (1953) also found that the major dissatisfaction was inadequate salary, and factors related to the disproportionate number of women on the teaching staff.

It is very unfortunate that the scales of pay of teachers are lower than other categories of employees who possess similar or even lower qualifications, experience and responsibilities, observed by Perumal (1969). He added that such a disparity promotes an unhealthy and undesirable competition and as a result, teachers become a disgusted and a dissatisfied lot.

According to Brown (1973) "An incentive is an objective goal which is capable of satisfying what we are aware of subjectively as a need, drive or desire". So monetary incentive or financial need or drive is one of the most and primary motives of work. Blum (1956) and Blum and Naylor (1968) states that in most of the studies financial incentives were found to be the most effective determinants of job satisfaction.

Annual Income

The influence of Annual Income on job satisfaction of Teacher Educators is studied. On the basis of annual income; the Teacher Educators are divided into three groups. Group 1 is formed with an annual income up to Rs. 100,000. Group 2 is formed with an annual income from Rs.100,001 to Rs. 200,000. Group 3 formed with an annual income Rs. 200,001 and above one way of ANOVA is employed, the results are presented in Table 5.15.

Table 5.15

Impact of annual income on job satisfaction

Sl. No.	Annual income (Rs.)	Number of observations	Mean	SD	'F' values	Level of significance
1.	Below 100,000	142	268.88	33.89	1.94	@
2.	100,001 to 200,000	239	273.89	35.44		
3.	200,001 to and above	211	276.49	37.29		

It is observed from table 5.15 that the computed value of 't' is 1.94 which is less than critical or table value (3.01) for 2 and 589 df at 0.05 level of significance. Hence, hypothesis 3 is accepted at 0.05 level. Therefore, it is concluded, the annual income of the Teacher Educators does not have significant effect on their job satisfaction.

Management

The impact of management on job satisfaction of Teacher Educators is studied. The Teacher Educators are divided into three groups based on the management where they are working. Group 1 is formed with the Teacher Educators working in minority colleges. Group 2 is formed with the Teacher Educators working in private colleges. Group 3 is formed with Teacher Educators working in government and university colleges. One-way ANOVA is employed, the results are shown in Table 5.16.

Table 5.16

Impact of management on job satisfaction

Sl. No.	Management	Number of observations	Mean	SD	'F' values	Level of significance
1.	Minority	172	271.64	34.92		
2.	Private	324	272.91	36.65	1.63	@
3.	Government	96	279.52	34.21		

It is clear from Table 5.16 the computed value of 'F' is 1.63 which is far less than the critical or table value of 'F' (3.01) 2 and 589 df at 0.05 level of significance. Therefore hypothesis 3 is accepted at 0.05 level. Hence, it is concluded that management of the B.Ed college does not have significant influence on job satisfaction of the Teacher Educators.

Suehr (1962) found that communication was one of the most vital areas in the whole moral process. It was most conspicuous by its absence, and consequently intended to be a major source of dissatisfaction. Sommers (1969) also observed that most of the teachers felt that there was a lack of communication between teachers and administrators.

Maheswar Panda (2002) conducted a study on job satisfaction of teachers in the contest of types of management. He found that there is no significant difference between government teachers and non- government teachers in respect of their satisfaction. And the college teachers, in general as well as both categories were satisfied with their job.

Total Members in the Family

The influence of total members in the family of the Teacher Educator on the job satisfaction is investigated. On the basis of total members in the family the Teacher Educators are divided into three groups. Group 1 is formed with the family members 6 and above. Group 2 is formed with the family members 4 and 5. Group 3 is formed with the family members upto 3. One way ANOVA is employed, the results are presented in Table 5.17.

Table 5.17

Influence of total members in the family on job satisfaction

Sl. No.	Total members in the family	Number of observations	Mean	SD	'F' values	Level of significance
1.	6 and above	149	273.93	38.59	0.35	@
2.	4 and 5	245	274.77	34.62		
3.	Up to 3	198	271.94	35.20		

It is evident from table 5.17 that the computed value of 'F' is 0.35 which is far less than critical or table value of 'F' (3.01) for 2 and 589 df at 0.05 level of significance. Hence, hypothesis 3 is accepted. It is concluded that total members in the family of Teacher Educator does not have significant influence on the job satisfaction.

Religion

The effect of Religion on the job satisfaction of Teacher Educators is investigated. Based on religion, Teacher Educators are divided into three groups. Group 1 is formed with Hindus. Group 2 formed with Muslim Teacher Educators. Group 3 formed with Christian Teacher Educators. One-way ANOVA is employed, the results are given in Table 5.18.

Table 5.18

Impact of religion on job satisfaction

Sl. No.	Religion	Number of observations	Mean	SD	'F' values	Level of significance
1.	Hindu	437	274.51	36.43	1.17	@
2.	Muslim	71	267.52	32.85		
3.	Christian	84	274.11	34.79		

It is observed from table 5.18 that the computed value of 'F' is 1.17. It is far less than critical or table value of 'F' (3.01) for 2 and 589 df at 0.05 level of significance. Hence, hypothesis 3 is accepted at 0.05 level. It is concluded that religion does not have significant influence on job satisfaction of Teacher Educators.

Caste

The effect of caste on job satisfaction of Teacher Educators is studied. The Teacher Educators are divided into three groups on the basis of caste. Group 1 is formed with scheduled caste (SC) and scheduled tribe (ST) Teacher Educators. Group 2 is formed with backward caste (BC), Teacher Educators. Group 3 is formed with open category (OC) Teacher Educators. One-way ANOVA technique is used and results are presented in Table 5.19.

Table 5.19

Impact of caste on job satisfaction

Sl. No.	Caste	Number of observations	Mean	SD	'F' values	Level of significance
1.	SC/ST	126	272.96	34.66	0.37	@
2.	OBC	225	275.21	37.52		
3.	OC	241	272.46	34.84		

It is clear from Table 5.19 that the computed value of 'F' is 0.37. It is for less than the critical or table value (3.01) of 'F' for 2 and 589 df at 0.05 level of significance. Therefore, hypothesis 3 is accepted at 0.05 level. Hence, it is concluded that caste does not have significant influence on job satisfaction of Teacher Educators.

INFLUENCE OF SELF-CONCEPT ON JOB SATISFACTION

The influence of 10 areas of self-concept and total score of self-concept on job satisfaction of Teacher Educators is investigated. The raw scores in each area of self-concept and also the total score on self-concept scale are separately obtained.

The frequency distribution of total score on the self–concept scale is presented in Table 5.20.

Table 5.20

The frequency distribution of total score on self-concept scale

S.No.	C.I	Limits	Mid Point	F	Cf	CPf
1.	131-140	130.5-140.5	135.5	3	3	0.50
2.	141-150	140.5-150.5	145.5	16	19	3.20
3.	151-160	150.5-160.5	155.5	73	92	15.54
4.	161-170	160.5-170.5	165.5	125	217	36.65
5.	171-180	170.5-180.5	175.5	135	352	59.45
6.	181-190	180.5-190.5	185.5	118	470	79.39
7.	191-200	190.5-200.5	195.5	84	554	93.58
8.	201-210	200.5-210.5	205.5	33	587	99.15
9.	211-220	210.5-220.5	215.5	4	591	99.83
10.	221-230	220.5-230.5	225.5	1	592	100.00

1. N	=	592		6. SD	=	15.36
2. MD	=	177.00		7. SK	=	0.01
3. MO	=	177.70		8. KU	=	2.66
4. R	=	97.00		9. CV	=	8.70
5. QD	=	11.00		10. SEM	=	0.63

There are 51 items in the self-concept scale. The minimum and maximum scores on the self-concept scale are 51 and 255 respectively. The neutral score is 153 (51 x 3). The mean total score of Teacher Educators on self-concept scale is 176.65. Therefore the Teacher Educators have positive self-concept. The values of skewness and kurtosis are 0.01 and 2.66 respectively. It is inferred that the distribution is slightly positively Skewed and lepto kurtic. It means that the scores are massed at low or left end of the scale, and are spread out gradually toward the high or right end of the scale.

The raw scores on each area of the self-concept and also the total score are converted into quartiles. On the basis of quartile values, the Teacher Educators, are divided into 3

Table 5.21

The values of M, SD, SEM, R, CV, Sk, and Ku for different areas of self concepts for the total sample

Sl.No.	Constructs	M	SD	SEM	R	CV	Sk	Ku
1.	Self-concept (A) (Health and sex appropria-teness)	22.08	3.46	0.14	16	15.70	0.01	2.55
2.	Self-concept (B) (Abilities)	29.90	5.00	0.20	27	16.72	0.14	3.04
3.	Self-concept (E) (Self confidence)	18.29	3.75	0.15	16	20.53	0.05	2.60
4.	Self-concept (F) (Self acceptance)	14.10	2.93	0.12	16	20.78	0.03	2.97
5.	Self-concept (H) (Worthiness)	26.34	3.96	0.16	28	15.06	0.31	3.47
6.	Self-concept (P) (Present, past and future)	16.82	3.57	0.14	19	21.22	0.04	3.17
7.	Self-concept (S_1) S1 (Beliefs and convictions)	10.95	2.35	0.09	11	21.48	0.19	2.59
8.	Self-concept (S_2) (Feeling of shame and guilt)	14.29	4.28	0.17	20	29.96	0.00	2.39
9.	Self-concept (S_3) (Sociability)	12.34	2.46	0.10	14	19.94	0.01	2.97
10.	Self-concept (SW) (Emotional)	11.48	3.78	0.15	16	32.91	0.03	2.40
11.	**Self-concept Total**	176.64	15.36	0.63	97	8.69	0.01	2.66

groups. Group 1 is formed with teachers up to Q1 (First quartile) Group 2 is formed with teachers above Q1 value and up to Q3 (Third Quartile). Group 3 is formed with Teacher Educators above Q3 value.

The values of M, SD, SEM, R, CV, Sk and Ku for different areas of self-concept and total score of self-concept for the total sample (N = 592) are presented in Table 5.21.

For all the areas and also for the total the values of skewness (Sk) are positive. It indicates that the scores are massed at the lower left end of the scale, and are spread out gradually toward the high or right end of the scale. The values of kurtosis (Ku) for the areas: 1. Health and sex appropriateness 2. Self confidence, 3. Self acceptance, 4. Beliefs and conductions, 5. Feeling of shame and guilt 6. Sociability, 7. Emotional, and 8. Self concept total are less than normal value (3.00). Hence the distributions are lepto kurtic. For the areas: 1. Abilities 2. Worthiness and 3. Present, past and future; the values of kurtosis (Ku) are more than the normal value (3.00). Hence the distributions are platy kurtic. All the values of Skewness (Sk) and Kurtosis

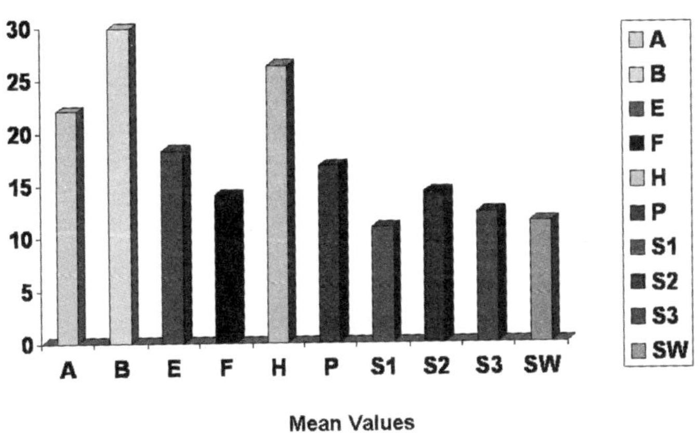

Graph 5.6. Bar diagram for the means of self-concept scores of Teacher Educators

(Ku) are very nearer to normal value. It is concluded that the distributions are very close to normal distribution.

The bar diagram for the means of self-concept scores shown in Graph 5.6.

The following Hypothesis is formulated

Hypothesis-4

There would be no significant influence of the different areas of self-concept and the total score of the self-concept on job satisfaction of Teacher Educators.

Hypothesis 4 is tested with the help of one way ANOVA and the results are shown from Table 5.22 to 5.32.

Table 5.22

Impact of self-concept A (Health and sex appropriateness) on job satisfaction

Sl.No	Group	Number of observations	Mean	SD	'F' ratio	Level of significance
1.	1	192	270.69	33.69	2.10	@
2.	2	291	273.36	36.17		
3.	3	109	279.45	38.08		

Table 5.23

Impact of self-concept B (Abilities) on job satisfaction

Sl.No	Group	Number of observations	Mean	SD	'F' ratio	Level of significance
1.	1	178	264.84	32.07	7.92	**
2.	2	302	276.89	35.57		
3.	3	112	278.72	39.72		

Table 5.24

Impact of self-concept E (Self confidence) on job satisfaction

Sl.No	Group	Number of observations	Mean	SD	'F' ratio	Level of significance
1.	1	187	271.80	35.57	1.06	@
2.	2	278	275.89	35.63		
3.	3	127	271.30	36.52		

Table 5.25

Impact of self-concept F (Self Acceptance) on job satisfaction

Sl.No.	Group	Number of observations	Mean	SD	'F' ratio	Level of significance
1.	1	174	267.62	33.10		
2.	2	300	274.87	35.37	4.14	*
3.	3	118	279.27	39.62		

Table 5.26

Impact of self-concept H (Worthiness) on job satisfaction

Sl.No.	Group	Number of observations	Mean	SD	'F' ratio	Level of significance
1.	1	184	267.91	36.38		
2.	2	269	275.89	33.29	3.44	*
3.	3	139	276.75	38.99		

Table 5.27

Impact of self-concept P(Present, past and future) on job satisfaction

Sl.No	Group	Number of observations	Mean	SD	'F' ratio	Level of significance
1.	1	187	270.06	34.71		
2.	2	267	273.29	35.98	2.52	@
3.	3	138	279.04	36.83		

Table 5.28

Impact of self-concept. S1 (Beliefs and convictions) on job satisfaction

Sl.No	Group	Number of observations	Mean	SD	'F' ratio	Level of significance
1.	1	156	273.76	33.62		
2.	2	366	272.67	36.93	0.71	@
3.	3	70	278.24	34.68		

Table 5.29

Impact of self-concept S2 (Feeling of same and guilt) on job satisfaction

Sl.No.	Group	Number of observations	Mean	SD	'F' ratio	Level of significance
1	1	156	269.63	34.60	1.49	@
		292	274.32	34.49		
		144	276.50	39.41		

Table 5.30

Impact of self-concept S3 (sociability) on job satisfaction

Sl.No.	Group	Number of observations	Mean	SD	'F' ratio	Level of significance
1.	1	206	271.75	36.03	0.50	@
2.	2	262	274.15	33.60		
3.	3	124	275.58	39.89		

Table 5.31

Impact of self-concept Sw (emotional) on job satisfaction

Sl.No	Group	Number of observations	Mean	SD	'F' ratio	Level of significance
1.	1	194	271.32	35.82	0.60	@
2.	2	263	274.98	34.64		
3.	3	136	274.42	38.04		

Table 5.32

Impact of the total score of self concept on job satisfaction

Sl.No.	Group	Number of observations	Mean	SD	'F' ratio	Level of significance
1.	1	153	261.38	33.22	12.89	**
		292	276.85	33.69		
		147	279.91	39.52		

It is observed from tables 5.22 to 5.39 that the values of 'F' are not significant for the areas. 1. Health and sex appropriateness 2. Self-confidence, 3. Present, past and future, 4. Benefit and convictions, 5. feeling shame and guilt, 6. sociability and 7. emotional; at 0.05 level of significance for 2 and 589 df. The critical or table value of 'F' for 2 and 589 df at 0.05 level is 3.01. Therefore hypothesis 4 is accepted for the above areas of self-concept at 0.05 level of significance.

The values of 'F' for the areas; 1. self-acceptance and 2. worthiness are more than critical or table value (3.01) for 2 and 589 df' at 0.05 level of significance. Therefore hypothesis 4 is rejected at 0.05 level of significance. Hence it is concluded that the areas self acceptance and worthiness have significant influence on the job satisfaction of Teacher Educators.

For the area "abilities" and the self-concept total score values of 'F' are more than critical or table value (4.65) for 2 and 589 df at 0.01 level of significance. Therefore hypothesis 4 is rejected at 0.01 level. Hence, it concluded that the area abilities and the self–concept total score have significant impact on job satisfaction of Teacher Educators.

INFLUENCE OF PERSONALITY ON JOB SATISFACTION

The influence of 16 personality factors form-C on job satisfaction of Teacher Educators is investigated. The raw scores on each personality factor for the total sample (N = 592) is obtained. The values of M, SD, SEM, R, CV, ST and Ku for all the 16 personality factors are presented in Table 5.33.

It is clear from Table 5.33 that the values of skewness for all the 16-factors is positive for some of the factors the values of skewness (Sk) is zero. It implies that most of the distributions of the personality factors are very nearer to normal distribution. The values of Kurtosis (Ku) for all the 16 personality factors are very nearer to the normal value

Table 5.33

The values of M, SD, SEM, R, CV, Sk, and Ku for various personality factors

Sl.No.	Constructs	M	SD	SEM	R	CV	Sk	Ku
1.	Factor A (Aloof-warm, outgoing)	7.87	2.27	0.09	10	28.91	0.05	2.57
2.	Factor B (Dull–Bright)	4.54	1.75	0.07	8	38.62	0.00	2.68
3.	Factor C (Emotional – Mature)	8.20	2.48	0.10	10	30.31	0.21	2.59
4.	Factor E (Submissive – Dominant)'	5.28	2.31	0.09	10	43.77	0.15	2.45
5.	Factor F (Glue, silent–enthusiastic)	5.97	2.23	0.09	12	37.44	0.01	3.06
6.	Factor G (Causal – conscientious)	9.18	2.43	0.10	11	26.48	0.55	2.81
7.	Factor H (Timid-adventurous)	5.94	2.31	0.09	12	38.92	0.03	3.00
8.	Factor I (Tough – sensitive)	5.25	2.02	0.08	11	38.67	0.00	2.51
9.	Factor L (Trustful–suspecting) –	5.13	2.37	0.09	12	46.28	0.05	3.56
10.	Factor M (Conventional-eccentric)	5.50	2.48	0.10	11	45.19	0.08	2.59
11.	Factor N (Simple – sophisticated)	5.75	2.16	0.08	11	37.63	0.00	2.40
12.	Factor O (confident-insecure)	6.96	2.48	0.10	10	35.64	0.01	2.10
13.	Factor Q_1 (conservative–experimenting)	6.29	2.02	0.08	10	32.15	0.00	2.59
14.	Factor Q_2 (dependent-self sufficient)	5.48	2.06	0.08	10	37.82	0.00	2.58
15.	Factor Q_3 (un controlled-Self controlled)	7.20	2.22	0.09	10	30.91	0.00	2.36
16.	Factor Q_4 (stable –Tense)	6.49	2.47	0.10	11	38.16	0.01	2.31

(3.00), and hence, the distributions are very nearer to normal distribution.

The following hypothesis is formulated.

Hypothesis 5

There would be no significant influence of 16 personality factors on job satisfaction of Teacher Educators. To test the above hypothesis the total sample on each personality factor is divided into 3 groups. The raw scores are converted into sten (standard) values. On the basis of sten values, the Teacher Educators are divided into 3 groups. Group 1 is formed with sten values 1 to 4. Group 2 is formed with sten values 5 and 6. Group 3 is formed with sten values 7 to 10. The influence of each personality factor on job satisfaction of Teacher Educators is studied by employing one way ANOVA and the results are given from Tables 5.34 to 5.49.

The bar diagram for the means of personality factors of Teacher Educators is shown in Graph 5.7.

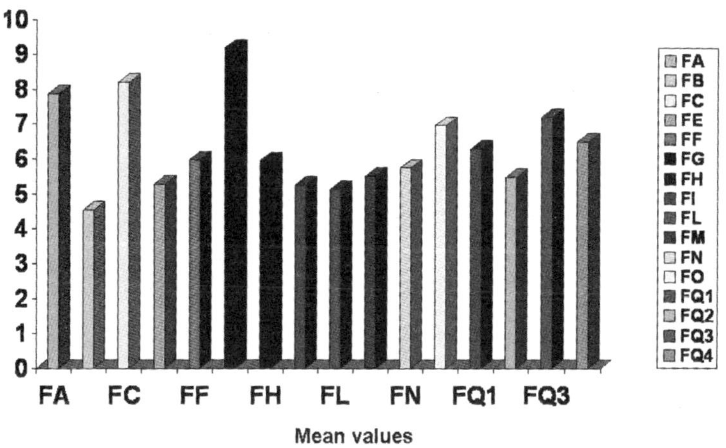

Graph 7. Bar diagram for the means of personality factors of Teacher Educators

Table 5.34

Influence of personality factor A on job satisfaction

S.No.	Group	Number of observations	Mean	SD	'F' ratio	Level of significance
1.	1	162	273.87	34.91	0.31	@
2.	2	275	272.50	35.33		
3.	3	155	275.32	37.69		

Table 5.35

Influence of personality factor B on job satisfaction

S.No.	Group	Number of observations	Mean	SD	'F' ratio	Level of significance
1.	1	159	270.33	34.85	0.44	@
2.	2	267	274.35	34.86		
3.	3	166	274.61	38.26		

Table 5.36

Influence of personality factor C on job satisfaction

S.No.	Group	Number of observations	Mean	SD	'F' ratio	Level of significance
1.	1	151	271.00	34.83	0.57	@
2.	2	232	274.09	36.34		
3.	3	209	274.97	35.58		

Table 5.37

Influence of personality factor E on job satisfaction

S.No.	Group	Number of observations	Mean	SD	'F' ratio	Level of significance
1.	1	255	273.81	36.18	1.76	@
2.	2	158	277.34	38.13		
3.	3	179	270.03	32.88		

Table 5.38

Influence of personality factor F on job satisfaction

S.No.	Group	Number of observations	Mean	SD	'F' ratio	Level of significance
1.	1	157	278.03	34.26	2.94	@
2.	2	300	270.17	36.92		
3.	3	135	276.14	34.51		

Table 5.39

Influence of personality factor G on job satisfaction

S.No.	Group	Number of observations	Mean	SD	'F' ratio	Level of significance
1.	1	135	268.71	35.98	1.64	@
2.	2	253	275.09	37.47		
3.	3	204	275.02	33.38		

Table 5.40

Influence of personality factor H on job satisfaction

S.No.	Group	Number of observations	Mean	SD	'F' ratio	Level of significance
1.	1	147	274.50	33.54	0.08	@
2.	2	290	273.06	34.78		
3.	3	155	273.81	39.79		

Table 5.41

Influence of personality factor I on job satisfaction

S.No.	Group	Number of observations	Mean	SD	'F' ratio	Level of significance
1.	1	230	275.47	35.63	0.73	@
2.	2	189	271.21	35.92		
3.	3	173	273.77	35.96		

Table 5.42

Influence of personality factor L on job satisfaction

S.No.	Group	Number of observations	Mean	SD	'F' ratio	Level of significance
1.	1	105	275.57	33.95	0.23	@
2.	2	340	273.49	35.88		
3.	3	147	272.51	37.10		

Table 5.43

Influence of personality factor M on job satisfaction

S.No.	Group	Number of observations	Mean	SD	'F' ratio	Level of significance
1.	1	196	274.59	36.80	0.27	@
2.	2	188	272.05	36.76		
3.	3	208	274.11	34.08		

Table 5.44

Influence of personality factor N on job satisfaction

S.No.	Group	Number of observations	Mean	SD	'F' ratio	Level of significance
1.	1	195	274.42	35.87	0.27	@
2.	2	167	274.53	33.58		
3.	3	230	272.26	37.40		

Table 5.45

Influence of personality factor O on job satisfaction

S.No.	Group	Number of observations	Mean	SD	'F' ratio	Level of significance
1.	1	184	271.75	37.85	2.59	@
2.	2	234	271.24	35.59		
3.	3	174	278.78	33.47		

Table 5.46

Influence of personality factor Q_1 on job satisfaction

S.No.	Group	Number of observations	Mean	SD	'F' ratio	Level of significance
1.	1	190	272.65	35.51	0.25	@
2.	2	221	273.18	36.11		
3.	3	181	275.16	35.90		

Table 5.47

Influence of personality factor Q_2 on job satisfaction

S.No.	Group	Number of observations	Mean	SD	'F' ratio	Level of significance
1.	1	214	274.99	36.09	0.33	@
2.	2	183	273.61	36.26		
3.	3	195	272.10	35.19		

Table 5.48

Influence of personality factor Q_3 on job satisfaction

S.No.	Group	Number of observations	Mean	SD	'F' ratio	Level of significance
1.	1	219	269.19	35.96	2.69	@
2.	2	182	275.81	35.90		
3.	3	181	276.63	35.18		

Table 5.49

Influence of personality factor Q_4 on job satisfaction

S.No.	Group	Number of observations	Mean	SD	'F' ratio	Level of significance
1.	1	209	276.89	35.58	2.80	@
2.	2	177	275.17	37.19		
3.	3	206	268.95	34.49		

It is evident from Table 5.34 to Table 5.49 that the computed values of 'F' for all the 16 personality factors are less than critical or table value (3.01) for 2 and 589 df at 0.05 level of significance. Therefore hypothesis 5 is accepted at 0.05 level of significance. Hence, it is conducted that the personality of the Teacher Educators do not have significant influence on their job satisfaction.

INFLUENCE OF JOB INVOLVEMENT

The raw scores for the total sample (N = 592) on job involvement inventory is obtained. On the basis of the raw scores the Teacher Educators are divided into 3 groups using quartiles. Group 1 is formed with raw score up to Q_1 (1st quartile) Group 2 is formed with raw score above Q_1 and up to Q_3 (3rd Quartile) and Group 3 formed with raw scores above Q_3.

The following hypothesis is framed.

Hypothesis 6

There would be no significant influence of job involvement on the job satisfaction of the Teacher Educators.

The above Hypothesis is verified using one way ANOVA and the results are shown in Table 5.50.

Table 5.50

Influence of job involvement on job satisfaction

S.No.	Group	Number of observations	Mean	SD	'F' ratio	Level of significance
1.	1	164	264.17	38.93		
2.	2	293	274.68	31.45	10.59	**
3.	3	135	282.78	38.20		

It is clear from Table 5.50 that the computed value of 'F' (10.59) for greater than the critical value or table value of 'f' (4.65) for 2 and 589 'F' at 0.01 level of significance. Therefore, hypothesis 6 is rejected at 0.01 level significance. It is concluded that the job involvement of Teacher Educators have significant influence on their job satisfaction.

MULTIPLE REGRESSION ANALYSIS

This section deal with the analysis of the relative contribution or magnitude of each of different independent variables to the dependent variable.

This analysis is presented in 4 parts. Job Satisfaction (JS) is the independent variable for all the parts. There are 42 variables for the purpose of regression analysis. 41 variables are independent and one variable (JS) is dependent. The variable number (VN), description of variable and symbol used are presented in table 5.51.

Table 5.51

Variables used in regression analysis

Variable No.	Description of the variable	Symbol used
1.	Sex	S
2.	Age	A
3.	Qualification	Q
4.	Teaching experience	TE
5.	Marital status	MS
6.	Occupation of spouse	OS
7.	Total salary per month	TM
8.	Annual income	AI
9.	Region	R
10.	Management	M
11.	Total members of the family	TM
12.	Religion	C
13.	Caste	CS
14.	Self concept A (Health and sex appropriateness)	SA
15.	Self concept B (Abilities)	SB

Variable No.	Description of the variable	Symbol used
16.	Self concept E (Self confidence)	SE
17.	Self concept F (Self acceptance)	SF
18.	Self concept H (Worthiness)	SH
19.	Self concept P (Present past and future)	SP
20.	Self concept S1 (Beliefs and convictions)	SS1
21.	Self concept S2 (Feeling of same and guilt)	SS2
22.	Self concept S3 (Sociability)	SS3
23.	Self concept SW (Emotional)	SW
24.	Self concept Total	SCT
25.	Factor A (Aloof-warm, outgoing)	FA
26.	Factor B (Dull –Bright)	FB
27.	Factor C (Emotional –Mature)	FC
28.	Factor E (Submissive –Dominant)	FE
29.	Factor F (Glue, silent –enthusiastic)	FF
30.	Factor G (Causal –conscientious)	FG
31.	Factor H (Timid- adventurous)	FH
32.	Factor I (Tough–sensitive)	FI
33.	Factor L (Trustful–suspecting)	FL
34.	Factor M (Conventional-eccentric)	FM
35.	Factor N (Simple–sophisticated)	FN
36.	Factor O (confident-insecure)	FO
37.	Factor Q_1 (conservative–experimenting)	FQ_1
38.	Factor Q_2 (dependent-self sufficient)	FQ_2
39.	Factor Q_3 (uncontrolled-Self controlled)	FQ_3
40.	Factor Q_4 (stable–Tense)	FQ_4
41.	Job Involvement	JI
42.	Job Satisfaction	JS

Variable number (VN) 42 that is JS in Table 5.51 is dependent variable and all the other 41 variables are independent in this investigation. Job satisfaction of Teacher Educators are so important for better student achievement. The Job satisfaction of Teacher Educator is related to so many variables like socio–demographic variables, self–concepts, personality etc.

Prediction of JS with the help of Socio-demographic Variables

The relative contribution of 13 socio–demographic variables (Variables 1 to 13 in table 5.51) to the dependent variable JS (variable 42 in Table 5.51) is investigated with the help of multiple regression analysis. The results of regression analysis are presented in Table–59.

It could be seen from Table 5.52 that only one variable out of 13 socio–demographic variables is entered into the regression analysis. The variable total salary per month (TM) is entered as only one variable into Stepwise multiple regression analysis. The multiple correlation (R) obtained is 0.077, indicating that the strength of the relationship between the two variables (JS and TM) is about 0.67 per cent. It could also be seen that R is significant. The critical of table value of 'F' for 1 and 590 'F' at 0.05 level is 3.86 and at 0.01 level is 6.69. The co-efficient of multiple R^2 is 0.007. This shows that 0.7 per cent of variance in JS is accounted by TM.

The standard error of multiple 'R' (SER) is 35.720. From this it may be inferred nearly 68 per cent of the actual JS value would lie within ± 35.720 points of JS value predicted with the help of this variable (TM).

The partial regression co-efficient (b) presented in column 7 is 5.13. This value indicates that JS value would change by 5.13 units for every unit of change in TM. The 't' value for 'b' is 1.99 which is significant at 0.05 level. The value of the constant that could be written to predict JS at this stage is 263.834.

Table 5.52

Prediction of Job Satisfaction score with the help of Socio-demographic variations

Sl. No.	1V (VN)	R	R^2	SER	F value for R	b (VN)	't' value for b	Constant	B	R	% of variance
1.	TM(7)	0.077	0.007	35.720	3.96* (1,590)	5.13(7)	1.99*	263.834	0.08	0.082	0.67

VN = Variable No.
IV = Independent Variable

The general form of the multiple regression equation may be written as

$$Y = A + b(X_1) + b_2(X_2) + b_3(X_3)......... + b_n(X_n)$$

Where Y is the predicted score on the dependent variable, A is a constant,

$b_1, b_2, b_3........b_n$ are partial regression coefficients and X_1, X_2, X_3———X_n are the scores of different independent variables.

Thus multiple regression equation at the end of this step could be written as:

JS = 263.834 + 5.13 (TM)

Prediction of JS with the help of Self-concepts

In this step-wise regression analysis 10 areas of self-concepts and total score of self-concept (Variables 14 to 24 in Table 5.51) are treated as independent variables and JS (Variable 42 in table 5.51) is treated as dependent variable. The effect of self concept on JS is investigated.

As the earlier case step-wise multiple regression analysis is carryout to assess the contribution of each of these independent variables to JS. The results obtained are presented in table 5.53.

In this step–wise multiple regression analysis, the first independent variable that entered is self–concept total score (SCT) that is variable 24 in table 5.51. The values of 'R' and R^2 at this stage are 0.178 and 0.032 respectively. Thus the amount of variance in JS explained by this variable is 3.24 per cent.

The multiple regression equation could be written as.

JS = 199.574 + 0.41 (SCT)

Self confidence (SE) is entered into the step-wise regression analysis as the second most significant variable. The multiple correlation (R) between JS on one side and SCT and SE on other side is 0.209. Thus the strength of relation- ship between JS and two independent variables

Table 5.53

Prediction of Job satisfaction score with the help of self-concepts

Sl. No.	1V (VN)	R	R^2	SER	F value for R	b (VN)	't' value for b	Constant	B	R	% of variance
1.	SCT (24)	0.178	0.032	35.254	19.74** (1,590)	0.41 (24)	4.44**	199.574	0.17	0.180	3.24
2.	SE (16)	0.209	0.044	35.071	13.56*** (2,589)	-0.56 (24) -1.18 (16)	5.20** 2.67**	159.904	-0.24 -0.12	- 0.005	4.35 0.06
3.	SS2(21)	0.216	0.047	35.040	9.73** (3,588)	0.64 (24) -1.26 (16) -0.54 (21)	5.29** 2.81** 1.42@	191.095	0.27 -0.13 -0.06	0.043	-4.95 0.06 -0.28

SCT and SE put together is about 21 per cent. R is significant at 0.01 level (F = 13.56 for 2 and 589 df).

The value of R^2 is 0.044. This shows that the variables put together could explain 4.4 per cent of variance in the dependent variable viz, J.S. Out of this 4.35 per cent of variance is explained by SCT and the remaining 0.06 per cent of variance is accounted by SE (Table 5.53, column 12).

The regression equation to predict JS with these two variables as predictor variables could be return as.

JS = 195.904 + 0.56 (SET) - 1.18 (SE)

There are only 3 variables out of 11 self-concept variables contributed to predict JS. These 3 variables are 1. self concept total score, (SET) 2. Self Confidence and (SE) and 3. Feeling shame and guilt. (SS_2). All these three Self-concept variables could explain 4.73 per cent of variance in JS.

The regression equation at the end of 3rd step is

JS = 191.095 + 0.64 (SCT) - 1.25 (SE) – 0.54 (SS_2).

Prediction of J.S. with the help of Personality Factors

In this analysis 16–personality factors (variables 25 to 40 in table 5.51) are treated as independent variables and JS (Variable 42 in Table 5.51) as dependent variable. The effect of 16 personality factors on JS is studied. As in the earlier case step-wise multiple regression analysis is carried out to assess the contribution of each of the independent variables to the score of JS. The results obtained are presented in Table 5.54.

In the step-wise regression analysis the 1st independent variable that entered is factor Q_4 (FQ_4). The multiple R obtained is 0.104. It is significant (F = 6.84) at 0.01 level for 1 and 590 'F'. The R^2 is 0.011.

Therefore, it could be informed that 1.1 per cent of the variance in JS is contributed by this variable. The partial regression coefficient (b) is -1.54. It is significant at 0.01 level. This shows that the changing JS is by -1.54 units for

Table 5.54

Prediction of Job satisfaction score with the help of personality

Sl. No.	1V (VN)	R	R^2	SER	F value for R	b (VN)	't' value for b	Constant	B	R	% of variance
1.	FQ4(40)	0.104	0.011	35.633	6.84** (1,590)	-1.54 (40)	2.61**	283.657	-0.10	-0.107	1.15
2.	FO (36)	0.130	0.017	35.557	5.20** (2,589)	-1.58 (40) 1.10 (36)	2.69** 1.88@	276.209	-0.11 0.07	0.073	1.18 0.56
3.	FG (30)	0.144	0.021	35.508	4.35** (3.588)	-1.62 (40) 1.06 (36) 0.97 (30)	2.75** 1.80@ 1.62@	267.794	-0.11 0.77 0.06	0.066	1.20 0.54 0.43

every unit of change in factor Q_4. The regression equation could be written as:

$$JS = 283.657 - 1.54 (FQ_4)$$

The second most important predictor variable that entered into the step-wise regression analysis is factor Q (FO) that is variable No.36. The values of R and R^2 at this stage are 0.130 and 0.170 respectively. Thus the amount of variance in JS explained by these two variables in combination is 1.7 per cent. Out of this, the contribution of FQ_4 is 1.18 per cent. The remaining 0.56 per cent of variance is contributed by FO.

The multiple regression equation with these the predictor variables FQ_4 and FO could be written as.

$$JS = 276.209 - 1.58 (FQ_4) + 1.10 (FQ)$$

There are only three steps in this regression analysis. The third predictor variable that entered into the Step-wise regression analysis is factor G (FG). The values of R and R^2 at this stage are 0.144 and 0.021 respectively. Thus the amount of variance in JS explained by these three variables in combination is 2.1 per cent. Out of this the contribution of FQ_4 is 1.20 per cent. The contribution of FO is 0.54 per cent. The remaining 0.43 per cent of variance is contributed by FG. The multiple regression equation at the end of 3rd step could be written as:

$$JS = 267.794 - 1.62 (FQ_4) + 1.06 (FO) + 0.97 (FG)$$

Prediction of JS with the help of all the Variables in the Study

The relative contribution of 13 socio-demographic variables, 11-Self-concepts, 16-personality factors and job involvement to the depended variable (JS) is studied with the help of multiple regression analysis. The results obtained are presented in Table 5.55.

It could be seen from Table 5.55 that the 1st variable entered into the step–wise multiple regression analysis is job involvement (JI), (Variable No. 41 in table 5.51). The multiple correlation (R) obtained is 0.254, indicating that

Table 5.55

Prediction of Job satisfaction score with the help of all the variables in the study

Sl. No.	1V (VN)	R	R^2	SER	F value for R	b (VN)	't' value for b	Constant	B	R	% of variance
1	JI (41)	0.254	0.065	34.648	41.29** (1,590)	1.31(41)	6.42**	181.396	0.25	0.256	6.54
2.	SCT (24)	0.316	0.100	34.022	32.85** (2,589)	1.34(41) 0.43(24)	6.67** 4.67**	102.590	0.26 0.18	0.180	6.67 3.30
3.	SE (16)	0.333	0.111	33.848	24.49** (3,588)	1.33(41) 0.57(24) -1.13(16)	6.65** 5.49** 2.66**	99.731	0.25 0.24 -0.11	-0.005	6.63 4.43 0.06
4.	FQ4 (40)	0.344	0.119	33.710	19.97** (4,587)	1.30(41) 0.57(24) -1.15(16) -1.35(40)	6.53** 5.53** 2.70** 2.41*	110.521	0.25 0.24 -0.12 -0.09	-0.017	6.48 4.44 0.06 1.00
5.	Fo (36)	0.356	0.127	33.598	17.07** (5,586)	1.33(41) 0.56(24) -1.08(16) -1.39(40) 1.13(36)	6.66** 5.50** 2.55** 2.49* 2.21*	100.163	0.25 0.24 -0.11 -0.09 0.08	0.073	6.60 4.40 0.05 1.03 0.63

Sl. No.	1V (VN)	R	R2	SER	F value for R	b (VN)	't' value	Constant for b	B	R	% of variance
6.	TM(7)	0.366	0.134	33.488	15.12**	1.34(41)	6.76**	89.295	0.26	0.082	6.68
					(6,585)	0.56(24)	5.42**		0.24		4.33
						-1.05(16)	2.50*		-0.11		0.05
						-1.36(40)	2.44*		-0.09		0.01
						1.31(36)	2.35*		0.09		0.66
						5.33(7)	2.19*		0.08		0.69
7.	FQ3(39)	0.370	0.137	33.448	13.33**	1.37(41)	6.86**	82,512	0.26	0.069	6.79
					(7,584)	0.54(24)	5.19**		0.23		4.17
						-1.03(16)	2.43*		-0.10		0.05
						-1.27(40)	2.27*		-0.08		0.94
						1.34(36)	2.41*		0.09		0.68
						5.57(7)	2.29*		0.08		0.72
						0.97(39)	1.55@		0.06		0.42

the strength of relationship between two variables (JS and JI) is about 25 per cent. It could also be seen that R is significant (F = 41.29) at 0.01 level for 1 and 590 df. The coefficient multiple R^2 is 0.065. This shows that 6.5 per cent of the variance in JS is accounted for by job involvement (JI).

The standard error of multiple R (SER) is 34.648 from this it may be inferred that nearly 68 per cent of the actual JS score would lie within ± 34.648. Points of JS scores predicted with the help of this variable.

The partial regression coefficient (b) presented in column 7 is 1.31. This value indicates that the JS scores would change by 1.31 units for every unit of change in JI. The 't' value for 'b' is 6.42 which is highly significant at 0.01 level (Column 8). The value of the constant that would go into the multiple regression equation that could be written to predict JS at this stage is 181.396.

Thus the multiple regression equation at the end of this step could be written as:

JS = 181.396 + 1.31 (JI)

Self-Concept total score (SCT, Variable 24) is entered into the step-wise regression analysis as the second most significant variable. The multiple correlation (R) between JS on one side and JI and SCT on the other side is 0.316. Thus the strength of relationship between JS and the two independent variables put together is about 32 per cent. R is significant at 0.01 level (F = 32.85).

The value of R^2 is 0.100. This shows that the two variables put together could explain 10.0 per cent of variance in the dependent variable, viz., JS. Out of this 6.67 per cent of variance is explained by JI and the remaining 3.30 per cent of variance is accounted for by SCT (Please see table 5.55, Col. 12).

The partial regression coefficients presented in col.7 show that when both JS and SCT are included as predictor variables, the JS would change by 1.34 and 0.43 points for every unit of change in JS and SCT respectively.

The partial regression coefficient of JS and SCT are significant at 0.01 level as shown in col. 8.

The regression equation to predict JS with these two variables (JS and SCT) as predictor variables could be written as:

$$JS = 102.590 + 1.34\ (JI) + 0.43\ (SCT)$$

There are 7 steps in this step–wise regression analysis. The regression equation at the end of 7th step could be written as:

$$JS = 82.512 + 1.37\ (JS) + 0.54\ (SCT) - 1.03\ (SE) - 1.27\ (FQ_4) + 1.34\ (FO) + 5.57\ (TM) + 0.97\ (FQ_3).$$

All the 7 independent variables put together could explain 13.7 per cent of variance in the depended variable (JS). The regression equation at the end of the 7th step would be the best to predict the dependent variable (JS).

A model of relationship between dependent variable and independent variables is shown in Figure 5.1.

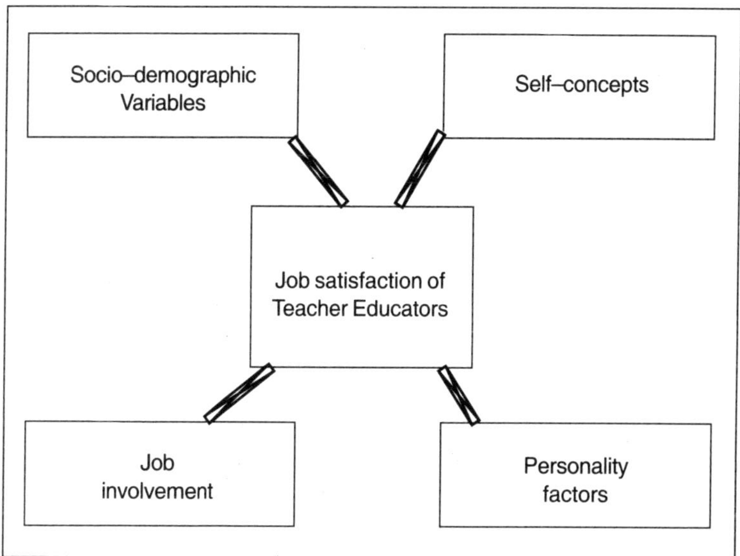

Fig. 5.1. A model of relationship between dependent variable and Independent variables.

CHAPTER 6

SUMMARY, FINDINGS, CONCLUSIONS, RECOMMENDATIONS AND SUGGESTIONS

This chapter deals with the summary, major findings, conclusions, recommendations and suggestions for further research.

SUMMARY

The Teacher Educators play an important role in any system of Education. No system of Education can ever rise higher than the level of the quality of its Teaching Profession. It is widely believed that creation of satisfactory working conditions would go a long way in increasing the efficiency of the persons involved in the process of Education. Hence, every country in the world has realized the need for improving the Teacher Educator's status, salaries, service conditions etc., and provide facilities for the pursuits of higher knowledge so that they can perform their duties more effectively. The Government of India and the State Governments are doing their best in this regard though there is much more to be done.

The Teaching Profession is at the lowest in the hierarchy of Professions. Today the most of the Teacher Educators express dissatisfaction with their profession in general and with many aspects of their job in particular. Therefore, there is great need for a study of a job satisfaction of Teacher Educators in relation to their job involvement, self-concept, personality factors and socio-demographic variables.

Statement of the Problem

The present study is concerned to look at whether Socio-demographic variables, self-concepts, personality and job involvement have any relation to the job satisfaction of the Teacher Educators working in B.Ed colleges. This study also intended to investigate whether it could be possible to predict the job satisfaction of Teacher Educators with the help of different sets of independent variables.

Title of the Problem

The Title of present investigation is, *"JOB SATISFACTION OF TEACHER EDUCATORS B.Ed COLLEGES"*.

Need for the Study

"No pupil can rise above the level of its teacher". The statement made about the role and status of Teachers in the National Policy and Education, 1986 is, besides bring commendable, an eye-opener to all of us who are engaged in the Teaching Profession. To provide quality Teacher Education at secondary level, Teacher Educators must maintain a high level of academic and professional competence so as to prepare the best teachers for our country's schools. Unless we Teacher Educators are in a position to provide worthwhile experiences to our pupil-teachers for realizing the stipulated Teacher Education objectives related to particular type of Teacher Education course, the talk of any worthwhile quality Teacher Education could be futile by all means, we have to illuminate ourselves like a lamp having enough energy in the form of burning oil for lighting the mind and hearts of our pupil-teachers.

Can we really play the role of such illuminated lamps? Are the present Teacher Educators available in our Teacher Education institution capable of providing the needed quality Teacher Education? Here an attempt is made to seek answer to these questions in the contest of the competence of our teacher educators working in B.Ed. colleges along with the existing conditions and practices available for educating them as Teacher Educators.

Teacher Educators have a key role in improvement of Education. Therefore, it is important that their best efforts be devoted to it. Since there is so much flexibility in the work they are required to do, and the manner in which they can do it, the contribution they make to the field depend in part on their involvement in their work and the satisfactions they derive from it. Hence, the investigator selected the satisfaction of Teacher Educators working in B.Ed colleges with respect of different variables.

Scope of the Study

The main object of the study is to draw the relationship of Job Satisfaction Scores of Teacher Educators belonging to different Sex, Region, Type of Management, Religion and Caste etc.

The study is also intended to test the impact of self-concepts, personality factors and Socio-Demographic variables on job satisfaction of Teacher Educators. The study is restricted to Teacher Educators working in B.Ed Colleges of Andhra Pradesh state only.

Objectives of the Study

The study has been designed with the following specific objectives:

1. To identify the level of job satisfaction of Teacher Educators working in B.Ed colleges.
2. To know the level of relationship of job satisfaction and job involvement of Teacher Educators.
3. To find the influence of sex and region on job satisfaction of Teacher Educators.
4. To know the interaction effect of sex and region on the job satisfaction of the Teacher Educators.
5. To find out the effect of socio-demographic variables on job satisfaction.

6. To find out the influence of self-concepts on job satisfaction.
7. To identify the influence of personality factors on job satisfaction.
8. To predict the job satisfaction with the help of different sets of variables namely socio-demographic variables, self-concepts and personality factors.
9. To predict the job satisfaction with the help of all the variables in the investigation.
10. To develop multiple regression equations in order to predict the job satisfaction of Teacher Educators.

Hypothesis of the Study

In the light of the above objectives, the following major Null hypotheses have been set up for the purpose of this investigation.

1. The Teacher Educators working in B.Ed colleges would not satisfy with their jobs.
2. There would be no significant relation between job satisfaction and job involvement of the Teacher Educators.
3. There would be no significant influence of the main effects Sex and Region on job satisfaction of Teacher Educators.
4. There is no significant interaction effect of sex and region on the job satisfaction.
5. Socio-demographic variables do not influence the job satisfaction of Teacher Educators.
6. Self-concept would not have significant influence on job satisfaction.
7. Personality of the Teacher Educators would not have significant bearing on job satisfaction.
8. It would not be possible to predict the job satisfaction of Teacher Educators with the help of the different

sets of variables namely socio-demographic variables, self-concepts and personality factors.

9. It could not be possible to predict job satisfaction with the help of all the variables in the investigation.
10. It could not be possible to develop the regression equations to predict job satisfaction with the help of independent variables of the present investigation.

Variables Studied

The present research problem involves investigation of Job Satisfaction of Teacher Educators working in B.Ed Colleges. The Job Satisfaction of Teacher Educators have been influenced by a number of Socio-Demographic and Psychological Variables are studied.

Dependent Variable

Job Satisfaction score is taken as the dependent variable for the study. The following aspects are considered for the development of job satisfaction inventory.

It is a 5- point attitude scale developed on lines suggested by Likert.

Independent Variables

The Independent Variables considered for the purpose of this investigation are 13 socio-demographic variables (Sex, Age, Educational Qualifications, Teaching Experience, Marital Status, Occupation of spouse, Total salary per month, Annual Income, Region, Management, Total members in the family, Religion and Caste).

10-self-concepts areas and total score of self-concepts, 16-personality factors and job involvement. Totally there are 41 independent variables.

Tools Used in the Study

The Tools used in present investigation are given below:

1. Job Satisfaction Inventory (JSI)

2. Job Involvement Inventory (JII)
3. Self Concept Scale (SCS)
4. Cattell's Personality Questionnaire (16 PF Form 'C')
5. Socio-Demographic Scale (SDS)

The validity and reliability of the above tools are established.

Sample Selected

The Sample for the investigation consisted of 592 Teacher Educators working in B.Ed Colleges in Andhra Pradesh. It is a stratified random sampling considered the aspects of Region and Sex.

Collection of Data

The investigator personally visited about 200 B.Ed. colleges in 3 regions of Andhra Pradesh state. After obtaining the permissions of the Head of the institutions the investigator personally met the Teacher Educators and explain the importance of the research problem. He distributed the research tools to the Teacher Educators and asked to return the filled-in questionnaire the very next day. If any Teacher Educator has not returned the filled-in questionnaire the investigator supplied the self-addressed stamp envelope and asked to send through postal service. Even if, the investigator is unable to receive the filled-in questionnaire through postal service, he once again sent the request reminder for receiving the filled-in questionnaire. Thus the investigator has taken meticulous care in collecting the research data.

Scoring and Analysis

The Job Satisfaction inventory was scored on 5-print scale by giving the weightages 5, 4, 3, 2, and 1 in the case of positive items and 1, 2, 3, 4, and 5 in the case of negative items. The total score of Job Satisfaction inventory is marked on the top right corner of the first page of the questionnaire. The same scoring procedure is followed for job involvement inventory. For self-concept scale and 16 PF questionnaire, the scoring key prepared by concerned authors used for socio–demographic scale, the numerical values are given for each variable to suit for the computer analysis.

The data is analysed with various perspectives based on the objectives of the study and hypotheses formulated for the study. Tables and graphs are used wherever necessary for presenting the data.

Statistical Techniques Employed

The analysis of data on job satisfaction scores of Teacher Educators working in B.Ed. colleges were carried out by computing the desriptive statistics such as measures of central tendency, measures of dispersion skewness, kurtosis, coefficient of variance and standard error of mean where ever necessary. Adequate number of tables and graphs were used for presenting the data. The inferential statistical techniques such as 't' and 'F'-Tests were employed to test different hypotheses. Multiple 'R' is calculated by carrying out step-wise regression analysis to predict the job satisfaction score of the Teacher Educators. The obtained numerical results were interpreted meaningfully.

MAZOR FINDINGS

The statistical treatment of the data reveals the following major findings of the study.

1. The Mean value of job satisfaction scores for the whole group (N=592) is 273.62 and median is 273.00. The Values of skewness and kurtosis are 0.04 and 2.55 respectively. These values of skewness and kurtosis are very nearer to the normal value that is 0.00 and 3.00. Hence the frequency distribution of job satisfaction scores is very close to the normal distribution. The maximum score that one can obtain on job satisfaction inventory is 400 (80 × 5) and neutral value is 240 (80 × 3). The mean value of job

satisfaction is greater than the neutral value and hence the Teacher Educators have better job satisfaction.

2. The frequency distribution of job satisfaction scores for Male and Female Teacher Educators are also very nearer to normal distribution. The mean score for Females and Males is 274.44 and 272.90 respectively.
3. The variables of Sex and Region do not have significant influence on job satisfaction of Teacher Educators. The two factor interaction namely Sex × Region also does not have significant influence on job satisfaction.
4. The socio-demographic variables viz; 1. Age, 2. Educational qualifications, 3. Teaching experience, 4. Marital status. 5. Occupation of spouse, 6. Salary per month, 7. Annual income, 8. Management, 9. Total members in the family, 10. Religion and 11. Caste do not have significant influence on job satisfaction of the Teacher Educators.
5. The self-concept area 'Abilities' and Total Score of Self-Concept have significant influence at 0.01 level on job satisfaction of Teacher Educators. The self-concept areas viz., 1. Self-acceptance and 2. Worthiness have significant influence on job satisfaction at 0.05 level. The remaining self-concept areas viz. 1. Health and Sex appropriateness, 2. Self confidence, 3. Present, past and future, 4. Beliefs and convictions, 5. Feeling of shame and guilty, 6. Sociability, and 7. Emotional do not have significant influence at 0.05 level on job satisfaction of Teacher Educators.
6. All the 16 Personality factors do not have significant influence on job satisfaction of Teacher Educators at 0.05 level of significance.
7. Job involvement has significant influence on job satisfaction of the Teacher Educators at 0.01 level of significance.

8. It is found that among the 13 socio-demographic variables only Total salary per month (TM) is contributing for the job satisfaction of Teacher Educators. It could be possible to explain 0.67 per cent of the variance in job satisfaction with the help of TM variables.
9. Among the 11 Self Concept variables only 3 variables namely Self-Concept total score (SCT), 2. Self Confidence (SE) and 3. Feeling of shame and guilt (SS_2) are contributing for the prediction of job satisfaction score of Teacher Educators. All these 3 variables put together could explain 4.7 per cent of variance in the job satisfaction score. The regression equation at the end of 3rd step is; JS = 191.095 + 0.64 (SCT) –1.25 (SE) – 0.54 (SS_2).
10. Among the 16 Personality Factors, only 3 factors namely 1. Factor-Q_4 (FQ_4), 2. Factor–0 (FO), 3. Factor–G (FG) are contributing to predict job satisfaction score. All the three personality factors put together explain 2.1% of variance in the job satisfaction score. The regression equation at the end of 3rd step could be written as: JS = 267.749 – 1.62 (FQ_4) + 1.06 (F_Q) + 0.97 (FG).
11. Among the 41 independent variables in the present investigation only 7 variables are contributing for the prediction of job satisfaction scores. They are 1. Job involvement (JI) 2. Self-Concept total score (SCT), 3. Self Confidence (SE), 4. Personality factor Q_4 (FQ_4), 5. Personality factor O (FO), 6. Total Salary per Month (TM) and 7. Personality factor Q_3 (FQ_3). All these 7 variables put together could explain 13.7 per cent of variance in the dependent variable namely job satisfaction scores. The regression equation at the end of the 7th step is:

    JS = 82.512 + 1.37 (JI) + 0.54(SCT) –1.03 (SE) –1.27 $FQ_{4)}$) + 1.34 (Fo) + 5.57 (TM) + 0.97 (FQ_3)

CONCLUSIONS

From the above findings the following conclusions are drawn.

1. The frequency distribution of job satisfaction scores of Teacher Educators working in B.Ed. colleges is very nearer to normal distribution.
2. On the whole the Teacher Educators are better satisfied with their job.
3. Sex has no significant influence on the job satisfaction of Teacher Educators.
4. Region has no significant influence on the Job satisfaction of Teacher Educators.
5. There is no interaction effect of Sex × Region on the job satisfaction of Teacher Educators.
6. All the Socio-demographic variables studied in this investigation do not have significant influence on the job satisfaction of Teacher Educators.
7. The self-concept areas 1. Abilities 2. Self-acceptance, 3. Worthiness, and 4. Total self-concept score have significant influence on the Job satisfaction of Teacher Educators.
8. All the 16 personality factors do not have significant influence on the Job satisfaction of Teacher Educators.
9. The Socio-demographic variables, self-concepts and personality factors independently do not contribute much for the prediction of Job Satisfaction score of the Teacher Educators.
10. Out of 41 independent variables in the study of the 1st and foremost independent variables for predicting Job satisfaction score is Job involvement (JI).
11. Among all the regression equations in the present investigation the following is the best to predict the job satisfaction score of Teacher Educators.

    $JS = 82.512 + 1.37\ (JI) + 0.54\ (SCT) - 1.03\ (SE) - .27\ (FQ_4) + 1.34\ (FO) + 5.57\ (TM)\ 0.97\ (FQ_3)$

EDUCATIONAL IMPLICATIONS AND RECOMMENDATIONS

The job satisfaction of an individual is most important for better outcome of any profession. For progress is the career of any individual job satisfaction place an important role. The job satisfaction will also depend on the degree of involvement in the day-to-day work of the job. On the basis of the results of the study the following educational implications and recommendations are made.

1. It is clear from findings that the some of the areas of self-concepts have significant influence on the job satisfaction of Teacher Educators. It is necessary to provide the adequate training for developing the self-concepts like 1. Abilities, 2. Self-acceptance, 3. Worthiness and 4. Self-concepts in general.
2. It is also found that job involvement has significant influence on the job satisfaction of the Teacher Educators. Necessary training may be provided for more job involvement of the Teacher Educators.
3. In service training programmes, workshops seminars etc. may be planned for increasing the job satisfaction of Teacher Educators.
4. We often hear that teachers are born but not made. Though it is a tribute to gifted and dedicated teachers. We should note that the number of such persons is limited. The success of any educational system depends mostly upon the teachers who implement them. He shapes the destiny of future citizens. It is he who lays the foundation for a happy and prosperous nation. He deserves reward, respect, reverence, recognition, honour and homage.
5. A satisfied and happy Teacher Educator is very likely to exert himself, work with enthusiasm and deliver the goods more efficiently and thereby make his pupils efficient, satisfied, enthusiastic and happy. Like wise a dissatisfied Teacher Educator is likely to make his pupils also dissatisfied in several respects.

Hence, the welfare of Teacher Educator should be of supreme concern to the educational administrators, the government and the society. Though the government has been doing moderately good work to enhance the prestige of the Teacher Educator by increasing the salaries, much remains yet to be done, as shown by the results of this investigation.

6. It was found that a majority of the Teacher Educators were dissatisfied with their job in general. It is well known that a dissatisfied teacher educator cannot perform his duty of teaching effectively. Hence the government and management of the private colleges should take up all possible steps to reduce the dissatisfaction vertically and control horizontally.

SUGGESTIONS FOR FURTHER RESEARCH

The following suggestions may be considered for further research on job satisfaction.

1. The study is restricted to job satisfaction of Teacher Educators working in B.Ed. colleges. It may be conducted for other Teacher Educators working in DIET's, Private Colleges, University departments of education etc.,
2. This study may also be conducted on teachers/ lecturers working in various schools and colleges.
3. This study is limited to the state of Andhra Pradesh. It may be extended to other states in India and also to other countries.
4. This is a Presage study wherein survey method is employed. Presage-Process-Product studies in the area of Job Satisfaction may be conducted.
5. Studies on job satisfaction in relation with job effectiveness may be conducted.
6. Studies on job satisfaction in relation with institutional complex may be conducted.

7. In measuring the personality of the Teacher Educators, at least two forms of 16 PF should be used to obtain more suitable results. But, in the present study only one form was employed because of the use of several other data gathering instruments. The further researchers may use at least two forms of 16 PF and the results may be compared.

BIBLIOGRAPHY

Adams, J.S., (1963); Toward an understanding of inequity, *Journal of Abnormal Psychology*, 67, 422-436

Adler, S., (1980); Self-Esteem and causal attributions for job satisfaction and dissatisfaction, *Journal of Applied Psychology*, 65, 3, 327-332.

Ahmed, S.H., (1984); A study of personal and job facets as determinants of job satisfaction for public senior high school teachers in the common wealth of Pennsylvania. *Dissertation Abstracts International*, 45, 5, 1580-A.

Al-Khaldi, A.M., (1983); Job content and context factors related to satisfaction and dissatisfaction in three occupational levels of the public sector in Saudi Arabia, *Dissertation Abstracts International*, 44, 5, 1917-A.

Altimus, C.A., and Tersine, R.J., (1973); Chronological area and job satisfaction : The young blue-collar worker. *Academy of Management Journal*, 16, 1, 56-66.

Altshuler, Thelma C.; Richter, Suzanne L. "Maintaining Faculty Vitality." New Directions for Community Colleges: Vol. 13, No. 4, pp. 49-61, December 1985

Anand , S.P. (1971); "Study of Teachers-pupil Relationship in Higher Secondary Classes in Delhi, Unpublished Ph. D. Thesis, University of Delhi.

Anand, S.P., (1977); School teachers: Job satisfaction *vs.* Extraversion and uroticism, *Indian Educational Review*, 12, 2, 68-78.

Anand, S.P., (1972); School teachers and job satisfaction, *Teacher Education*, 7, 1, 16-23.

Anjali (1995); "A socio-psychological study of self-concept of Dalit students," *Indian Journal of Psychological Abstracts*, August, 1997, Vol. 84, No. 8.

Anjaneyulu, B.S.R., (1968); A study of job satisfaction in the secondary school teachers and its impact on the education of pupils with special reference to the state of Andhra Pradesh, in *A Survey of Research In Education* (Ed). Buch. M.B. Centre of Advanced Study in Education, M.S. University, Baroda.

Armstrong, T.B. (1971); Job content and context factors related to satisfaction for different occupational levels, *Journal of Applied Psychology*, 55, 1, 57-65.

Aston, M.C., et al., (2004); A six-factor structure of personality-descriptive adjectives: Solutions from psychological studies in seven languages. *Journal of Personality and Social Psychology,* 86, 356-366.

Atteberry, M.G.(1977); The relationship between emotional stability and job satisfaction of elementary school principals". *Dissertation abstracts international*, 37(1), 6163-A.

AVA: (1948), *American Vocational Association research bulletin* No. 3, "Factors Affecting the Satisfaction of Home Economics Teachers," Committee on research publications. AVA Inc., Washington, D.C.

Balakrishna Reddy, P. (1990); "Job satisfaction of primary school teachers". Unpublished M.Phil. dissertation, submitted to Sri Venkateswara University, Tirupati.

Balasubramaniam, S., and Narayanan, S., (1977); Effect of Personality on Job Satisfaction among college teachers, *Journal of Educational Research and Extention,* 13, 191-194.

Bange, E.J., (1944); How to learn what workers think of job and boss, *Factory Management and Maintenance*, 102, 5, 101-104.

Baron, R. (1986); *Behavior in organizations.* Newton, MA: Allyn and Bacon.

Bass, B.M. (1965); *Organizational Psychology,* Allygn and Bacon, Boston.

Becvar, R.J., (1969); "Job satisfaction of first year teachers, A study of Discrepancies between expectations and experiences," Unpublished Doctoral Dissertations, University of Minnesota.

Belasco, J.A. and Alutto, J.A., (1972); Decisional participation and teacher satisfaction, *Educational Administration Quarterly,* 8, 1, 44-58.

Benoit, S.S., (1977); "Job satisfaction among faculty women in Higher Education in the State Universities of Louisiana", *Dissertation Abstracts International*, 6969-A.

Berk, L.E. (1996); *Child development* (Third Edition), New Delhi, Illinois State University, Prentice Hall of India Private Limited.

Bernard, N. and Kulandaivel, K. (1976); "A study of hob satisfaction among graduate teachers in coimbatore. *Journal of Educational Research and Extension*, 13, 120-124.

Best, J.W., (1948); *Research in Education,* Prentice-Hall International Inc., Englewood Cliffs. N. J.

Bhuyan, B. (2005); Job satisfaction among college Teachers; *Asian Journal of Psychology and Education,* Vol. 38, No. 1-2, 29-32.

Bidwell, C.E., (1959); The Administration and Teaching Satisfaction, phi Delta Kapan, 37, 258-288.

Bindu, C.H., (2007); "Relationship between job satisfaction and stress coping skills of primary school teachers." Edutracks Vol. 6, No. 5.

Birmingham, J.A., (1985); Job satisfaction and burnout among Minnesota teachers, *Dissertation Abstracts International,* 45, 8, 2318-A.

Blai, Jr. B., (1982); "Predicting job satisfaction", *ERIC,* Vol, 17(5). Document Reproduction Service No. ED. 210582.

Blan. P.M. (1986); *Formal organization: A comparative study approach,* Sanfrancisco, Chansly, intext.

Blandford, S., Grundy, W., (2000); Developing a culture for positive behaviour management. *Emotional and Behav Difficulties* 19(1): 21-32.

Blauner, R.M., (1963); *Psychology of Personal in Business and Industry,* Printice Hall, Englewood Cliffs, N.J., New Jersey.

Blum, M.L., and Naylor, J.C., (1968); *Industrial Psychology and its Social Foundations,* Harper and Row, New York.

Blum, S.M., (1961); The desire for security, *Journal of Education Psychology,* 52, 317-321.

Boyd, B.J., Schneider N.I., (1997); Perceptions of the work environment and burnout in Canadian child care providers. *J. Res. Childhood Educ.* 11(2): 171-180.

Bradburn, N.H., (1969); The Fundamental Social Psychological Well-being, Aldine, Chicago, 147-179.

Brayfield, M.L., and Crockett, W.H., (1955); Employee attitudes and employee performance, *Psychological Bulletin,* 52, 392-424.

Brouwers, A., Tomic, W., (2000); A longitudinal study of teacher burnout and perceived self-efficacy in classroom management. *Teaching and Teacher Educ* 16(2): 239-253.

Brown, F., (1973); The job satisfaction of administrators within a multi-ethnic steeing , *ERIC,* Vol. 8., Document Reproduction Service No. Ed. 90645.

Bulter, T.M., (1961); Satisfaction of Beginning Teachers. *Clearing House,* 36, 11-13.

Burke, R.J., Greenglass, E., (1993); Work stress, role conflict, social support, and psychological burnout among teachers. *Psychol Rep* 73(5): 371-380.

Byrne, B.M., (1991); The Maslach Burnout Inventory: Validating factorial structure and invariance across intermediate, secondary and university educators. *Multivariate Behav. Res.* 26(4): 583-605.

Byrne, B.M., (1994); Burnout: Testing for the validity, replication, and invariance of causal structure across elementary, intermediate and secondary teachers.

Caldwell, Corrinne (1986); "Community College Faculty Careers." Paper presented at the Annual Meeting of the American Educational Research Association (San Francisco, California, April 15, 1986). 29 p. (ED 269 112).

Carrell, M.R. and Elbert, N.F., (1974); Some personal and organizational determinants of job satisfaction of postal clerks, *Academy of Management Journal,* 17, 2, 368-372.

Carrol Bryan Shannon, (2001); Co-operating Teaching Parison Students Teachers. The Center for Education, Widene University, Chester, pp. 499-512.

Castro, N.L., (1986); "Working class women, The relationship of job characteristics and job involvement to psychological well-being in employed mothers." *Dissertation Abstracts International, May* 83.47(11), 3978-A.

Cattell, R.B. (1990); "Advances in Cattellian personality theory" in L. A. Pervin (Ed.), *Handbook of Personality: Theory and Research,* New York: Guildford. (pp. 101-110).

Cattell, R.B., (1946); *The Description and Measurement of Personality,* World, New York.

Cattell, R.B., (1950); The main personality factors in questionnaire, self-estimated material, *Journal of Social Psychology,* 31, 3-38.

Chen, W.S., (1977); The job satisfaction of school teachers in the Republic of China as related to personal and organizational characteristics, *Dissertation abstracts international* 38, 6, 3167-A.

Clagett, Craig A., (1980); "Teacher Stress at a Community College: Professional Burnout in a Bureaucratic Setting." *Largo, Md: Prince George's County Community College*, 60p. (ED 195 310).

Cohen, Arthur M., Brawer, Florence B., (1982); The American Community College. San Francisco: Jossey-Bass

Cohen, M.A., (1977); The job consciousness of public school teachers: A case study of work ideology in Newton, Masschusetts, *Dissertation Abstracts International,* 37, 9, 5471-A.

Conn, S.R., & Rieke, M.L., (1994); The 16PF Fifth Edition Technical Manual. *Champagne,* IL: Institute for Personality and Ability Testing, Inc.

Cornell, Dewey G., et al., (1995); "Achievement and self-concept of minority students in Elementary school gifted programs", *Journal of the education for the Gifted, (Win) cited in Psychological abstracts,* Vol. 83, No. 9.

Costello, J.M. and Lee, S.M., (1974); "Need fulfillment and job satisfaction of professionals", *Public Personnel Management,* 3(5), 454-461.

Counts, G.E., (1978); Senior teachers: An endangered species. *ERIC,* Vol. 13. Document Reproduction Service No. ED 159132.

Coverdale, G.M., (1973); "Some determinants of teacher morale in Austrila, *Educational research* 16 (1), 34-39

Crites, J.O., (1961); Factor analytic definitions of vocational motivation, *Journal of Applied Psychology,* 45, 330-337.

Daly, R.E., (1981); A causal analysis of satisfaction, performance, Work environment and leadership in selected secondary schools. *Dissertation Abstract International,* 42, 2, 472-A.

Davis, F.G.T., (1981); Secondary teachers satisfaction– dissatisfaction: A symbolic interactionist analysis. *Dissertation Abstract International,* 42, 2, 645-A.

De Heus P, Diekstra RFW (1999); Do teachers burn out more easily? A comparison of teachers with other social professions on work stress and burnout symptoms. In: Vandenberghe R, Huberman AM (eds).

Derek Rowntru (1981); *"A Dictionary of Education",* Harper & Row Publishers, London, pp. 276, 288.

Dinham S, Scott C (2000); Moving into the third outer domain of teacher satisfaction. *J. Educ. Admin.* 38(4): 379-396.

Dobge, J.M., (1983); Perceived organizational and personal factors related to job satisfaction in public school teachers, *Dissertation Abstract International,* 44, 5, 1730-A.

Dorman, JP, (2003); Relationship between school and classroom environment and teacher burnout: A Lisrel analysis. *Social Psychol. Educ.* 6(2): 107-127.

Elloy, C.J., Bhomer, M and Kliff, N.D. (1991); The range of changing the attitude towards Job involvement, *Journal of Applied Psychology,* 28, p. 38.

Englhardt, V., (1973); Teacher's job satisfaction in schools of different levels. *Journal of Psychologic in Enziehung and Untirricht,* (In) *Psychologic Abstracts,* 52, 11974.

English, H.B., (1934); *A Students dictionary of psychological terms* (4th ed), Harperand Row, New York.

Ewen, R.B. et al., (1966); "An Empirical test of the Hergberg Two-factor theory', *Journal of applied psychology,* 50,544-50.

Eysenck, H.J., & Eysenck, M. W. (1985); *Personality and individual differences: A natural science approach.* New York: Plenum.

Faris, J.P., (1977); A study of the determinants of job satisfaction *Dissertation Abstract International,* 37(10), 6163-A.

Fenech, M., (2006); The impact of regulatory environments on early childhood professional practice and job satisfaction: A review of conflicting discourses. *Aust. J. Early Childhood* 31(2): 49-57.

Festinger, L., (1957); *A Theory of Cognitive Dissonance,* Evanston, III; Row, Peterson.

Filan, Gary L.; Okun, Morris A.; and Witter, Robert A. (1986); "Influence of Ascribed and Achieved Social Statuses, Values, and Rewards on Job Satisfaction among Community College Faculty." *Community / Junior College Quarterly of Research and Practice*: Vol. 10, No. 2, pp. 113-122.

Form, W.H., (1946); "Toward an occupational social psychology", *Journal of social psychology,* 24, 85, 99.

Freeman, F.S. (1965); *Theory and practice of psychological testing, A text book,* Oxford and IBH publishing House Co., New Delhi, p. 37, 91.

Friedlander, F., (1963); Underlying sources of job satisfaction, *Journal of Applied Psychology,* 47, 4, 246-250.

Friedlander, Jack (1978); The Relationship Between General Job Satisfaction and Specific Work-Activity Satisfaction among Community College Faculty. *Community/Junior College Research Quarterly;* Vol. 2, No. 3, pp. 227-240.

Ganguli, H.C. (1964); *Structure Processes of Organization,* Asia Publishing House, Bombay-89.

Garre H.H.E., (1973); *Statistics in psychology and education,* A Text Book, Publishers Vikals, Feffar and Siman Pvt. Ltd., Bombay. Pp. 337-370.

Gartner, S., (1981); The States of the American public school teacher, 1980-81 *NEA (National Education Association) From news front of phi.Dete Kappan* 63 (9), 579

Gechman, A.S. and Wiener, Y., (1975); Jon involvement and satisfaction as related to mental health and personal time devoted to work. *Journal of Applied Psychology,* 60, 521-523.

Gellmon, W., (1939); The components of vocational adjustment, *Personnel Guidance Journal,* 31.

Gilford. J.P. (1954); *Psychometric methods A Text book,* McGraw-Hill publishing company, New York, pp. 373, 374, 398, 417.

Gobel, I.W. (1977); Relationships between job satisfaction, demographic factors, absenteeism and tenure of workers in a Delmarva broiler processing plant. *Dissertation Abstracts International,* 38, 1820-A.

Godkin, R.L., (1982); Anticipated job satisfaction: Attitudinal bias among university female business majors, *Dissertation Abstract International,* 43, 1, 211-A.

Goldberg, L. R., & Digman, J. M. (1994); "Revealing structure in the data: Principles of exploratory factor analysis." In S. Strack & M. Lorr (Eds.), *Differentiating normal and abnormal personality* (pp. 216-242). New York: Springer.

Good, C.V. (1973); *Dictionary of Education,* McGraw-Hill Book Company. New Delhi.,

Good, Barr, A.S. and Scates, (1941); *Methodology of educational research,* New York, Appletion century crafts, Inc., pp. 10-18.

Gordon, J.E., (1963); Review of R.B. Cattell's Personality and Social Psychology, *Contemporary Psychology,* 11, 236-238.

Gordon, P.A., (1981); A validation study of the theory of work adjustment: The prediction of teacher satisfaction, *Dissertation Abstract International,* 42, 1, 34-A.

Guilford, J.P., (1954); Psychometric methods, *Tata MacGraw – Hill Publishing Company,* Faridabad, Haryana, India.

Gupta, R.N., (1977); A study of the personality traits of primary school teachers, *Journal of Applied Psychology,* 55, 3, 259-286.

Gupta, S.P. (1974); *Statistical methods* : A text book, Sultan chand and Sons, New Delhi.

Gutman, L (1947); "A Basis for scaling of quantitative data", *American Social Review,* 9, pp. 130-150.

Hackman, J.R., and Lawler III, E.E., (1971); Employee reactions to job characteristics, *Journal of Applied Psychology,* 55, 3, 259-286.

Hackman, J.R., and Oldham, G.R., (1976); Development of the job diagnostic survey, *Journal of Applied Psychology,* 60, 2, 159-170.

Hall, C. S., & Lindzey, G. (1978); *Theories of personality* (3rd ed.). New York: Wiley.

Hall, C. S., Lindzey, G., & Campbell, J. B. (1998); *Theories of personality* (4th ed.). New York: Wiley.

Halpern, G., (1966): Relative contributions of motivator and hygiene factors to overall job satisfaction, *Journal of Applied Psychology,* 50, 198-200.

Harding. E. (1964); Characteristics of participants in an employee suggestion plan, *Personal Psychology,* 17, 289-303.

Harnish, Dorothy; Creamer, Donald G., (1985); "Faculty Stagnation and Diminished Job Involvement." Community College Review; Vol. 13, No. 3, pp. 33-39.

Hergberg, F, (1966); Work and nature of man, world, Cleveland, and Snyderman, B.B. 1959.*The Motivation to Work,* Willey, New York.

Herzberg, F., Mausner, B., Peterson, R.O. and Capell, D.F., (1957); *Job Attitudes: Review of Research and Opinion,* Psychological Services of Pittsburg, Pittisburg.

Hodge, C.M., (1977); An analysis of the attitudes regarding job satisfaction held by negro professiors and white professors in selected institutions of higher education desegregated since 1954, *Dissertation Abstract International*, 37, 11, 6976-A.

Holdaway, E.A., (1978); Fact and overall satisfaction of teachers. *Educational Administration Quarterly,* 14, 1, 30-47.

Hoppock, R. (1935); *Job satisfaction,* Harper and Bros., New York.

Horn, J. (2001); Raymond Bernard Cattell (1905-1998). *American Psychologist, 56,* 71-72.

Hughes, H.M., (1972); Vocational choice, level and consistency: An investigation of Holland's theory on an employed sample, *Journal of Vocational Behavioru,* 2, 4, 377-388.

Hulin, C.L., (1977); "Satisfactions and other job attitudes". (In) Wolman, B.B., (Ed). *International Encyclopedia of Psychiatry, Psychology, Psychoanalysis and Neurology,* Vol. 10. (SA-ST). Aesculapius Publishers, Inc., New York.

Hulin, C.L., and Smith, P.C., (1964); Sex differences in job satisfaction, *Journal of Applied Psychology,* 48, 2, 88-92.

Hull, R.L. and Kolstad, A. (1942); Morale on the job. (In) Watson, Goodwin (ed) *Civilian Morale*, Reynal & Hitchcock Inc., New York, 349-354.

Hutton, Jerry B. (1985); Jobe, Max E. "Job Satisfaction of Community College Faculty." *Community / Junior College Quarterly of Research and Practice:* Vol. 9, No. 4, pp. 317-324 1985.

Inlow, G.M., (1951); Job satisfaction of Liveral arts graduates, *Journal of Applied Psychology,* 35, 175-181.

John Bellingnham (2004); Academic Dictionary of Education Academic Publishers, *New Delhi,* pp. 165, 166, 227, 314.

John, O. P. (1990); "The Big Five factor taxonomy: Dimensions of personality in the natural language and in questionnaires." In L. A. Pervin (Ed.), *Handbook of Personality: Theory and Research* (pp. 66-100). New York: Guildford.

John, O. P. (1999); "The Big Five trait taxonomy: History, measurement, and theoretical perspectives." In L. A. Pervin & O. P. John (Eds.), *Handbook of personality: Theory and research* (2nd ed., pp. 102-138). New York: Guildford.

Johnson, E.D. (1967); "An Analysis of factory related to teachers, Satisfaction and dissatisfaction." Unpublished doctoral Dissertation, A urban university. *Abstracted in Psychological Abstracts,* 54, pp. 375-393.

Jorde-Bloom P (1986); Teacher job satisfaction: A framework for analysis. *Early Childhood Res.* Q 1(2): 167-183.

Kalanidhi, M.S. (1973); Problem of job satisfaction among women worker in industry. In Shanmugham,T.E.(Ed), University of Madras. India

Kantas, A, Vassilaki E. (1997); Burnout in Greek teachers: main findings and validity of the Maslach Burnout Inventory. *Work & Stress* 11(1): 94-100.

Kates, S.L., (1950); Rorschach responses, straning blank scales, and job satisfaction among policemen, *Journal of Applied Psychology,* 34,4, 249-254.

Katz and Khan, R.L. (1966); *The Social Psychology of organizations,* Willey, New York.

Katzel, R.A., (1964); Personal values, job satisfaction and job behaviour," (In) Borow, H (Ed.), 1964, *Man in a world at work,* Houghton miflin Company: Boston. 341-363.

Kaurgu, G.K., (1981); An investigation of job satisfaction-dissatisfaction among elementary school teachers and head teachers in Nairobi, Kenya, And a comparison of their perceptions on fourteen selected job factors from Herzberg's two-factors Theory, *Dissertation Abstracts International,* 42, 1, 38-A.

Kavanagh, M.J. and Halpern, M. (1970); The impact of job level and sex differences on the relationship between life and job satisfactions. *Academy of Management Journal,* 20, 66-73.

Kentle, J.V.L., (1985); A follow up study of industrial education doctoral graduates of the period of 1972 through 1982 to investigate the degree of job satisfaction. *Dissertation Abstracts International,* 45, 2421-A.

Ketzell, R.A., (1964); "Personal values, Job satisfaction and job behaviour", in borrow, H., (ed) *Man in a world of work,* Houghton, Mifflin company, Boston.

Kilbridge, M.D., (1961); Turnover, absence and transfer rates as indicator a employee dissatisfaction with repetitive work. *Industrial and labour relation Review,* 15, 21-32.

Kilpatrik, H.W., (1949); "Modern Education and Better Human relations-Anti-Deformation League of B' Nai B'rith".

Kirkpatrick, R.N. (1962); "The Relationship of Job satisfaction to perceived staff promotional policies; found in Robinson, H.A. and Cannors, R.P. 1963, *Job satisfaction Researches. Personal and Guidance J.*, 42, pp.136-142.

Koeske, G.F., Koeske R.D., (1989); "Construct validity of the Maslach Burnout Inventory: A critical review and reconceptualization." *The J. Appl. Behav. Sci.* 25(2): 131-144.

Koustelios, A., (2001); Personal characteristics and job satisfaction of Greek teachers. *The Int. J. Educ. Manage* 15(7): 354-358.

Koustelios, A., Bagiatis, K. (1997); The employee satisfaction inventory (ESI): development of a scale to measure satisfaction of Greek employees. *Educ., Psychol. Meas.* 57(3): 469-476.

Koustelios, A., Kousteliou. I, (1998); Relations among measures of job satisfaction, role conflict, and role ambiguity for a sample of Greek teachers. *Psychol Rep* 82(1): 131-136.

Koustelios, A. Tsigilis, N. (2005); Relationship between burnout and job satisfaction among physical education teachers: A multivariate approach. *Euro. Phys. Educ. Rev.* 11(2): 189-203.

Kreitner and kinicki; (1998); *Organizational behaviour*. New York. McGraw Hill.

Krishna Reddy, N. (1976); Job satisfaction of teachers in relations to some variables like sex, locality, personality, etc. Unpublished M.Ed. dissertation, S.V. University, Tirupati.

Kuhn, B.J., (1982); Teacher personality type and job satisfaction, *Dissertation Abstracts International,* 43, 1, 104-A.

Lamb, K. (1997); Raymond Bernard Cattell: A lifetime of achievement. *Mankind Quarterly,* 38, 127.

Larsen, R.J., & Buss, D.M. (2002); *Personality psychology: Domains of knowledge about human nature.* New York: McGraw-Hill.

Lawler, and Hall, D.T. (1970); Relationship of job characteristics of job involvement, satisfaction and intrinsic motivation. *Journal of Applied Psychology,* 54, 305-312.

Lawler, and Porter, L.W. (1967); The effect of performance on job satisfaction. *Industrial Relations,* 7, 20-28.

Lawler, E.E., (1971); III Pay and Organisational Effectiveness : *A Psychological View,* McGraw-Hill, New York.

Lawler, E.E. III. (1965); *The mythology of management compensation.* Mimeographed Yale University, New Haven, Conn.

Lease, S. (1998); Annual review, 1993-1997: Work attitudes and outcomes. *J. Vocational Behav.* 53(2): 154-183.

Lee, R.T., Ashforth, B.E. (1993); A further examination of managerial burnout: Toward an intergraded model. *J. Organizational Behav.* 14(1): 3-20.

Lewis, A.L.F., (1982); Job satisfaction, decisional discrepancy, academic social climate and academic achievement in selected title I elementary schools, *Dissertations Abstracts, International,* 43, 1, 35-A.

Likert, R., (1932); "A Technique for the measurement of Attitudes", in Bragfield, A.H. and Rothis, H.F. 1951, *An Index of Job Satisfaction, Applied psychology,* 35(5) pp. 307-311.

Locke, E.A., and Whiting, R.J., (1974); Sources of satisfaction and dissatisfaction among solid waste management employees, *Journal of Applied Psychology,* 59, 2, 145-156.

Lodhal, and Kejner, M. (1965); The definition and measurement of job involvement. *Journal of Applied Psychology,* 49, 24-33.

Lodhal, T.M. (1964); Patterns of job attitudes in two assembly technologies. *Administrative Science Quarter,* 8, 484-519.

Loher, B.T., Noe, R.A., Moeller, N.L., and Fitzgerald, M.P., (1985); A Meta-Analysis of the relation of Job characteristics to Job Satisfaction, *Journal of Applied Psychology,* 70, 2, 280-289.

Madhu Raj (Ed): (1996); *Encyclopeadic Dictionary of Psychology and Education,* Anmol Publications Pvt.Ltd. New Delhi, Vol.1& 3, pp. 8, 210, 211, 1482, 1765, 178.

Maghradi, A. (1999); Assessing the effect of job satisfaction on managers. *Int. J. Vaule-Based Manage* 12(1): 1-12.

Mahesewar Panda, (2002); A study of job satisfaction of teachers in the context of types of management. *The Educational Review,* Vol. 45. No.4, pp. 16-19.

Maheswar Thaker, (2007); Correlates of job satisfaction of secondary school principals in Bhavnagar district. *Experiments in Education* pp. 13-15.

Mangal, S.K. (2002); *"Statistics in Psychology and Education", A* text book, Second edition, prentice- Hall of India Pvt. Ltd., New Delhi.

Mangal, S.K. (1982); *Educational Psychology.,* A text book, Prakash Brothers, Educational Publications, Ludhiyana. India, pp. 283-286.

Manlove, E. (1993); Multiple correlates of burnout in child care workers. *Early Childhood Res.* Q 8(4): 499-518.

March, J.G., and Simon, H.A., (1958); *Organisations*, Wiley, New York.

Marr, E and Mathur, R.K. (1973); Job satisfaction of teacher educators. *Indian Educational Review,* 8, 10-20.

Maslach, C. (1999); Progress in understanding teacher burnout. In: Maslach C, Jackson S (1986); *Maslach burnout inventory manual.* Palo Alto: Consulting Psychologists Press.

Maslach C, Leiter MP (1999); Teacher burnout: A research agenda. In: Maslach C, Schaufeli WB, Leiter MP (2001); *Job burnout. Ann Rev Psychol* 52: 397-422.

Maslow, A.H., (1943); "A Theory of Human Motivation". *Psychological review*, 50, 370-396.

McNemen Q. (1962); *Psychological statistics.* 3rd ed. New York, John Wiler.

McCanaughy, J.B., and Palmer, J.D., (1969); Personality and performance of federal field executives in South California, *Public Personel Review,* 30, 4, 205-210.

Mishra, Y.N., (1972); Stresses and strains of secondary school teachers, *Educational India,* 38,218-221.

Mokry, A-I (1981); Job Satisfaction in the education industry: A case study of teachers' interaction conditions which work in high school, *Dissertation Abstracts International,* 42, 1, 355-A.

Morse, N.C., (1953); *Satisfactions in White Collar job* (Annual report. Michigan Institute for Social Research, University of Michigan). 72.

Morse, N.C., Weiss, R., and Griggs, R., (1954); Attitudes toward work. Unpublished study. Institute for social research, (University of Michigan, Ann Arbor, (in) Bum and Maylor (1968), *Industrial Psychology,* Harper & Row, New York.

Myers, M.S., (1964); Who are Your Motivated Workers? *Harvard Business Review,* 42, 1, 73-88.

Nalini, K. (2004); Job satisfaction primary school teachers. Unpublished M.Ed.. Dissertation. S.V. University, Tirupati.

NCERT, (1970); *A study of reactions of teachers towards teaching profession,* Data Processing and Education Unit, NIE, New Delhi.

NEA., (1957); *The Status of American Public School Teacher,* National Education Association Research Bulletin, 35.

Neelakandan R., Rajendran K., (2007); Job satisfaction of public sector employees. *Journal of community guidance & Research* Vol. 24. No. 2, pp. 115-120.

Neeraja Dwivedi and Pestonjee, D.M., (1975); Socio-Personal correlates of job satisfaction, *Psychological studies,* 20, 2, 30-49.

Noller, P., & Law, H., & Comrey, A. L. (1987); The Cattell, Comrey, and Eysenck personality factors compared: More evidence for five robust factors? *Journal of Personality and Social Psychology,* 53, 775-782.

Orden, S.R., and Bradburn, N.M., (1968); Dimensions of marriage happiness, *American Journal of Sociology,* 73,715-732.

Oshagbemi, T. (1999); Academics and their managers: a comparative study in job satisfaction. *Personnel Rev* 28(1/2): 108-123.

Padmanabhaiah, S. (1984); "Job satisfaction and teaching effectiveness of secondary school teachers." Unpublished Ph.D. dissertation, Sri Venkateswara University, Tirupati.

Panda, B.N. (1999); Attitude towards teaching and work values, *The Primary Teacher,* No. Vol. XXIV, January 1999.

Parasiva Murthy, C.N., (1966); "A study on job satisfaction of workers in an industry concern in Hubli", *The Journal of Karnatak University, Social sciences,* 2, 158-162.

Patnaik, S.P. and Panda, K.C. (1982); Personality and attitude patterns of good and poor teachers working in secondary schools. *Journal of Education and Psychology,* 39(4), 232-240.

Peruman, V., (1969); Teachers' status, *The Education Quarterly,* 21,15-18.

Pervin, L. A., & John. O. P. (2001); *Personality theory and research* (8th ed.). New York: Wiley.

Pestonjee, D.M., (1973); Organisational structures and job attitudes, (in) Neeraja Dwivedi and Pestonjee, D.M., 1976, Off-the-job factors and job satisfaction: Some evidence for the inter actional model, *Psychological Studies,* 21,2,11-14.

Pestonjee, D.M., and Singh, A.P., (1973); Morale of first-level supervisors, *Indian Journal of Social Work,* 4, 3, 189-193.

Porter, L.W., (1961); 'A Study of perceived need satisfaction in bottom and middle management Jobs', *Journal of Applied Psychology,* 45, 1-10.

Porter, L.W., (1962); Job attitudes in management, Perceived deficiencies in need fulfillment as a function of job level, *Journal of Applied Psychology,* 46,375-384.

Porter, L.W., and Lawler, E.E., III, (1965); Properties of organizational structure in relation to job attitudes and job behaviour,' *Psychological Bulletin,* 64, 23-51.

Prasad, K. (2003); "A study of Job satisfaction of high school teachers," unpublished M.Ed Dissertation. S.V. University. Tirupati

Rajagopalam, K.R. and Rajaraman, P.G. (1977); "Teacher—what do they think", *New Frontiers in Education.* 7 (4), 56-62.

Rajagopalam, S., (1976); Measurement of teaching success. *Experiments in Education,* 3 and 4, 1976.

Ramakrishnaiah, D. (1980); "A Study of job satisfaction, attitude towards teaching and job involvement of college teachers," M. Phill. Dissertation, submitted to Sri Venkateswara University, Tirupati.

Rao, G.R.S. (1970); Socio-personal correlates of job satisfaction. *Indian Journal of Applied Psychology,* 2, 63-70

Riday, George, E., Bingham, Ronald D.; and Harvey, Thomas R. (1985); "Satisfaction of Community College Faculty: Exploding a Myth." Community College Review: Vol. 12, No. 3, pp. 46-50.

Robert, H. (1990); A study of selected factors related to Job satisfaction in the staff organization of large southern Baptist Churcher, Welch, *Dissertation Abstracts International,* 51,1974-A.

Robinowitz, J.D. and Hall, G.R. (1977); Teachers Belief systems and preschool atmosphere *Journal of Educational Psychology,* 55, 341-345.

Robinson, (1959); 'Job Satisfaction researches of 1958' *Personal and guidance journal,* 37, 669-73.

Robinson, H.A., and Hoppock, R, (1952); Job satisfaction Resume of 1951', *Occupations,* 30,594-98.

Rohland BM, Kruse GR, Rohrer JE (2004); Validation of a single-item measure of burnout against the Maslach Burnout Inventory among physicians. *Stress & Health* 20(2): 75-79.

Rossier, J., de Stadelhofen, F. M., & Berthound, S. (2004); The hierarchical structures of the NEO-PI-R and the 16 PF 5. *European Journal of Psychological Assessment*, 20, 27-38.

Salch, S.D., and Otis, J.L., (1964); Age and level of job satisfaction, *Personnel Psychology*, 17,425-430.

Sarveswara Rao, G.V., (1972); Intrinsic and extrinsic factors in job satisfaction of male clerical employees, *Psychological Studies,* 17,1,45-52.

Schaufeli WB, Dierendock DW (1995); A cautionary note about the cross-national and clinical validity of cut-off points of the Maslach Burnout Inventory. *Psychol. Rep.* 76(3): 1083-1090.

Schmidt, G.L., (1976); Job Satisfcation among secondary school administrators, Educational *Administration Quarterly,* 12, 2, 68-86.

Schuerger, J.M., Zarella, K.L., & Hotz, A.S. (1989); Factors that influence the temporal stability of personality by questionnaire. *Journal of Personality and Social Psychology,* 56, 777-783.

Schwartz, M.M., Jenusaites, E., and Stark, H., (1963); Motivational factors among supervisors in the utility industry, *Personnel Psychology,* 16, 45-53.

Scott, W.E., (1966); "Activation Theory and Task Design", *Organisational Behaviour and Human Performance,* 1, 3-30.

Seenivasan , C. (2007); Job satisfaction of higher secondary school teachers. *Journal of community guidance and research,* Vol. 24, No. 2, 163-172.

Sergiovanni, T.J., (1975); Financial incentives and teacher accountability: are we paying for the wrong thing? *Educational Administration Quarterly,* 11, 2, 112-115.

Sharma. Y.P., (2005); A study of job satisfaction among the physical education teachers working in Himachal Pradesh schools. *Indian Educational review* Vol. 41. No. 2.

Shaver, H.C., (1977); Job satisfaction, career patterns and job hunting among journalism graduates, *Dissertation Abstracts International,* 37, 11, 6817-A.

Sheppard, H.L. and Herrick, N.O., (1974); *Where have all the robots gone? Worker dissatisfaction in 1970;* Free Press, New York.

Shirom A, Ezrachi Y (2003); On the discriminant validity of burnout, depression and anxiety: A re-examination of the burnout measure. *Anxiety, Stress and Coping* 16(1): 83-97.

Siegel, L., (1969); *Industrial Psychology,* Richard, D., Irwin, inc., Home Wood, Illinois, 331-362.

Singh, P.N., and Wherry, R.J., (1963); Ranking of job factors by factory workers, *Indian Journal of Social Work,* 26, 1-6.

Sinha, D., and Nair, R.R., (1965); A study of job satisfaction factory workers, *Indian Journal of Social Work,* 26, 1-6.

Sinha, D., and Sarma, K.C., (1962); Union attitudes and job satisfaction of Indian workers, *Journal of Applied Psychology,* 46, 247-251.

Sinha. D. and Aggarwal, R., (1971); A study of job satisfaction in factory workers, *Indian Journal of Social Work,* 26, pp. 1-6.

Smith, H.D., (1982); Teacher voluntary absenteeism and perceptions of the professional environment, job satisfaction and impact of collective bargaining, *Dissertation Abstracts International,* 43, 1, 41-A.

Smith, J.J., (1977); Job satisfaction of Connecticut Public Senior High School Principals as related to school location and school size, *Dissertation Abstracts International,* 37, 9, 5517.

Smith, P.C., Kendall, L.M., and Hulin, C.L., (1969); *The Measurement of Satisfaction in Work and Retirement,* Rand McNally, Chicago.

Sommers, N.L., (1969); "Factors influencing teachers Morale in selected secondary schools", unpublished doctoral dissertation, State University, Kent.

Srole, L., Langer,. T., Standley, M., Marvin, O., and Thomas, R., (1962); Mental Health in the Metropolis: *The Midtown Man Hattan Study,* McGraw-Hill: New York, 177-178.

Ssidneysiegal (1956); *"Non-Parametric statistics for the Behavioural sciences",* Mc Graw Hill book Co., Inc., New York.

Stagner, R., Flabee, D.R., and Wood, E.A., (1952); Working on the Railboard: A study of job satisfaction, *Personnel Psychology,* 5, 293-306.

Sterba, J. (2000); *Ethics: Classical Western texts in feminist and multicultural perspectives.* New York: Oxford University Press.

Stockford , L.O., and Kunze, K.R., (1950); Psychology and the pay cheque, *Personnel,* 27, 129-143.

Stremmel AJ, Benson MJ, Powell DR (1993); Communication, satisfaction, and emotional exhaustion among child care center staff: Directors, teachers, and assistant teachers. *Early Childhood Res Q* 8(2): 221-233.

Sucher, J.H. (1962); A study of Morale in Education utilizing in complete sentences, *Journal of Educational Research,* 56,75-81.

Suchitra. D., (2003); Job satisfaction of women employed in various occupations. *Journal of community guidance and research,* Vol. 20, 237-244.

Sukla Roy Choudary (Das) (2007); Professional awareness vis-à-vis job satisfaction of college and university teachers in Assam. *Edu Tracks* Vol. 6-IV, 7.

Surbida, M.M. (1984); A study of the Job satisfaction of elementary principals, *Dissertation Abstract International,* 45(3) 1010.

Tabatabai, H.A., (1981); A comparative study of job satisfaction and internal-external locus of control in private and public organizations, *Dissertation Abstracts International*, 42, 2, 780-A.

Taneja, R.P. (1991); "Dictionary of Education", 2nd Edition, New Delhi; *Anmol Publications,* pp. 44, 183.

Togia A, Koustelios A, Tsigilis N (2004); Job satisfaction among Greek librarians. *Library and Inf. Sci. Res.* 26(3): 373-383.

Uma, S. (1984); Job and Life satisfaction experienced by, Dal Career family members, *Journal of Psychology, Researchers,* 28(3)139-144.

Usmani, S.N. et al., (2006); Teachers job satisfaction in relation to their personality type and types of school. *Edutracks.* Vol.6, No.3.

Van Dick R, Wagner U (2001); Stress and strain in teaching: a structural equation approach. *Br. J. Educ. Psych.* 71(2): 243-259.

Vandenberghe, R, Huberman, AM, (2001); *Understanding and preventing teacher burnout: A sourcebook of international research and practice,* Cambridge University Press: Cambridge UK, pp. 211-222.

Venkata Rami Reddy, A. (1984); Postgraduate students want a change over to internal assessment. *Asian Journal of Psychology and Education,* 13.

Venkata Rami Reddy, A. and Babjan, O. (1980); Why do teachers working in government and private schools differ in the level of their job satisfaction? *Journal of Educational Research and Extension,* 17, 65-74.

Venkata Rami Reddy, A. and Krishna Reddy, N. (1978); Job satisfaction of teachers working under different managements. *The Educational Quarterly,* 30, 28-29.

Venkata Rami Reddy, A. and Krishna Reddy, N. (1980); Are teachers satisfied with their jobs? A study. *Journal of Indian Education,* 6-57-65.

Venkata Rami Reddy,A. and Ramakrishnaiah, D. (1981); Job satisfaction of teachers. *Journal of Education and Psychology,* 38, 211-218.

Venkata Rami Reddy, A. (1972); "A study of the vocational needs of secondary pupils (Boys) in relation to their occupational choices and other variables." Unpublished Ph.D. thesis, S.V. University Tirupati.

Vijayalakshmi Ghali, (2005); Teacher effectiveness and job satisfaction of women teachers. *Edutracks.* Vol. 4, No. 7.

Vijayalakshmi, A. (1985); "Opinion of adult education instructors about their profession and adult education in general." Master dissertation, S.V. University, Tirupati.

Vroom V.H., (1964); *Work and Motivation,* Wiley: New York.

Wanous, J.P., and Lawler, E.E.III., (1972); Measurement and Meaning of job satisfaction, *Journal of Applied Psychology,* 56,(2), 95-105.

Weaver, C.N., (1974); Correlates of job satisfaction: some evidence from the national surveys, *Academy of Management Journal,* 17, 2, 373-375.

Weaver, C.N., (1977); Relationships among pay, race, sex, occupational prestige, supervisory work, autonomy and job satisfaction in a national sample, *Personnel Psychology,* 30, 437-466.

Weiner, A.M., (1981); Sex role preference and job satisfaction among secondary Home Economics teachers, *Dissertation Abstracts International,* 42, 2, 580-A.

Weinroth, E.D., (1977); Motivation, Job satisfaction, and career aspirations of married women teachers at different career stages, *Dissertation Abstracts International,* 38,6,3206-A.

Weitz, J., and Nuckolos, R.C., (1955), Job satisfaction and job survival, *Journal of Applied Psychology,* 39, 274-300.

White, K. (1996); The Relationship of Career involvement to persistence in the teaching profession among beginning female elementary teachers, *Journal of Educational Psychology,* 60. pp. 51-53.

Whitebook M, Phillips D, Howes C (1993); *National child care staffing study revisited.* Oakland, CA: Child Care Employee Project.

Williams, L.K., (1965,); Some Correlates of risk taking. Personnel Psychology, 18, 297-309.

Winer, B.J. (1971); *Statistical principals is experimental design,* A Text Book, McGraw-hill Book Co., New York.

Wolman, B.B., (Ed)(1977); International Encyclopedia of Psychiatry, Psychology, Psycho-analysis and Neurology, Vol. 10 (SA-ST), Aesculaplus Publishers, Inc., New York.

Wood, D.A. (1974); Effect of worker orientation differences on job attitude correlates. *Journal of Applied Psychology,* 59(1), 54-60.

Yate, M.W. (1965); *Statistics an Education and Psychology. A text book, the McMillan Co. New York.*

'Statistical Analysis in Educational Research' by Lind Quist, F.F., (1940).

'Statistical Works for Research Workers' by Fisher (1950).

'Fundamentals Statistics in Psychology and Education' by Guilford (1950)

'Statistics in Psychology and Education' by Henry E., Garrett and R.S Wood Worth (1961)

'Statistics in Education and Psychology' by Yate (1965)

'Statistical Principles in Experimental Design' by Edwards (1971)

'Experimental Design in Psychological Research' by Edwards (1971)

'Statistics in Psychology and Education' by Garrett (1973)

'Statistical Methods' by Gupta (1974)

'Applied Regression Analysis' by Draper and Smith (1981)

'Statistics in Psychology and Education' by Mangal (2002);

www.wikipedia.com-free online encyclopedia.

http://www.personalityresearch.org/papers/fehringer.html

INDEX

M

N

O

P